PRAISE FOR

Bloomin' Adventures

"Tim Gannon has led a magnificent life. He is a winner in international business, a champion in international polo, a steady and reliable hand on a dive boat, and a hell of a cook — and this is only the beginning."
— **Tommy Lee Jones**

"I knew Tim Gannon was a real food connoisseur right from the start! When I first met him, all we talked about was food, food, food, so much so that we jumped on a helicopter to fly down to the Florida Keys and landed right at the Islamorada Fish Company to eat fried key lime pie. And it was delicious!!
The whole time up and back, all we talked about was food and when we're going on the next adventure.
So, on our next adventure, we went to New Orleans and met the Super Magic Chef himself. Ate at the greatest restaurant, had a concert, and flew back to Palm Beach. It doesn't get any better than this.
Now, when is our next adventure, Tim? I'm getting hungry just writing this! LOL"
— **Robert Van Winkle**, aka Vanilla Ice

"Tim is far more than a great friend. He stood by my side during one of the most difficult moments of my career, when loyalty meant everything. Together, we shared unforgettable victories and won the most important tournaments in the world. These are memories I will carry with me forever."
— **Adolfo Cambiaso**
10-Goal Polo Player

"Tim, from winning the Silver Cup together in Florence to lining up at Tidworth against King Charles, I have seen firsthand the life you have built and the way you have built it. Nothing about it was accidental. You have always had a way of seeing opportunity where others see nothing, finding your 'Velcro' in an onion and turning it into something extraordinary. But what has always meant the most to me is who you are beyond the wins: endlessly curious, deeply knowledgeable, and incredibly generous. This book is your journey, but to those of us who know you, it is exactly the life we have watched you create."
— Salvatore Ferragamo

"Without Tim's diligence in making sure that Bloomin' Onion became successful, I doubt Outback would have become the huge success it became."
— Chris Sullivan
Co-Founder, Outback Steakhouse

"Tim has one of the biggest hearts you'll ever encounter — and I should know, because he stole mine thirty years ago. He is, without question, the kindest and most compassionate person I have ever known. He moves through the world with a perspective entirely his own, seeing possibilities where others see limits, always searching for a way to turn a 'no' into a 'yes.' He was pretty diligent to earn that first date, yes, from me, and I'm grateful every day that he did. His determination is fearless, his drive is inspiring, and he loves with a boldness and depth that few possess. To know Tim is to love Tim."
— Shannon Falcone

"We were sixteen when we met, and I think we both knew, somehow, that this one was different. Over the decades that followed, I came to understand what that feeling meant. Tim does not just dream; he builds worlds, and if you are lucky enough to stand close to him, those worlds become yours, too.
Years after our handshake deal between friends, the phone rang. It was Tim. "I am honoring my handshake deal with you," he said. "Come to Florida. We are going to build our polo team." I hesitated, but my wife, Shelley, did not. "We have to go," she said. I closed my

law practice, packed up my family, and we went, and I have never once looked back.

The world sees the legend: the Bloomin' Onion, the restaurants, the championships. I know the man behind it all: the most quietly generous human being I have ever met. He gives without announcement, without applause, and without needing a single soul to notice. That is the purest form of grace I have ever witnessed up close.

We are different in all the right ways. Tim sees the horizon; I find the path. He ignites the fire; I tend the flame. After all these years, I can only say this: some people come into your life and expand it. Tim did not just expand mine; he transformed it. He is like a brother and the best friend anyone could ever have."

— Phil Heatley

"When I think about my dad, a lot of memories come to mind, but the one that stands out most is how much I look up to him. He is a great dad because he is always thinking of others before himself. Even when it isn't easy, he chooses kindness. He has sacrificed so much so I could grow up with opportunities he never had and the love of a strong family. I hope that someday I can be even half the father to my children that he has been to me."

— JT Gannon

Son of Tim Gannon

"His legacy is measured not only by the victories he earned, but by the people he lifted along the way. As his son, I watched him build winning teams in business and on the polo field with a rare ability to bring out the very best in those around him. His words could energize any room, and his vision pushed people to think, and live, far beyond what they thought possible. He traveled the world without maps, guided by instinct and a deep belief in people, forming genuine connections everywhere, from the grooms who cared for the horses to the kings of nations. Wherever his path led, he left behind stronger people, bigger dreams, and a lasting sense of what was truly possible."

— Chris Gannon

Son of Tim Gannon

BLOOMIN' ADVENTURES

The Partners, the Risks, and the
Recipe Behind Outback Steakhouse

Bloomin' Adventures: The Partners, the Risks, and the Recipe Behind Outback Steakhouse

Library of Congress Control Number: 2026911033

Gannon Press: Wellington, Florida
Produced and published by Deyson Ortiz / Gannon Press
Written with Don Yaeger
Cover Design by Brent Spears
Copy editing, interior design, and typesetting by St. Petersburg Press

This is a work of nonfiction. The events and experiences described herein are true and have been faithfully rendered as the author remembers them, to the best of his ability. Some names, identities, and details have been changed to protect the privacy of the individuals involved.

ISBN:979-8-9949363-0-6

First Edition, 2026
10 9 8 7 6 5 4 3 2 1

BLOOMIN' ADVENTURES

The Partners, the Risks, and the Recipe Behind Outback Steakhouse

by Tim Gannon
with Don Yaeger

For Phil Heatley, who showed me a dream worth chasing and a friendship worth keeping.

For Chris Sullivan, who reached into the dugout when I was at my lowest and put me on the field. For the first time, I truly belonged, and before long, I felt like I was part of the World Series.

If a 15-year-old tying rebar in Louisiana dirt can help build Outback Steakhouse, play polo with a future king, and win his final match at Palermo with his son at his side, then your dream is closer than you think.

This book took me five years to write, and I wanted to make it something special for you.

My hope is that you enjoy the adventures and the journey, and that you carry something from these pages with you long after you have finished reading.

Any dream is within reach if you work hard, stay focused, believe in yourself, and surround yourself with the right partners. Anything is possible.

Enjoy the Bloomin' Adventures.

— Tim Gannon

Co-founder, Outback Steakhouse
Creator of the Bloomin' Onion

Preface

You are holding more than a book. You are holding proof that the life you dream of is within reach.

I am that proof.

My mother raised six children alone. We were not wealthy. I started selling newspapers at nine. At fifteen, I spent a summer in New Orleans, digging pool ditches and tying steel rebar under a sun that never let up. By sixteen, I was parking cars at a restaurant until well past midnight.

I remember one afternoon in particular. I was at the bottom of a pool ditch, covered in mud, my hands raw from the wire. The heat pressed down. I had no direction, no plan, no sense of where my life was headed.

I looked around and asked myself if this was all there was.

That day, I decided it was not.

Not long after, my best friend took me to see something I had never experienced before. I cannot describe what happened, only that everything changed. In a single afternoon, I found my why: the dream that would drive every decision I made for the next fifty years.

It seemed impossibly out of reach. A world for the wealthy, not for a teenager delivering newspapers and parking cars. But I could not let it go. The dream had chosen me.

From that day forward, every risk I took, every sacrifice I made, and every hour I worked was in service of one thing. I did not build a career to get rich. I built it to fund the life I wanted to live.

That pursuit carried me from those pool ditches to something I still have trouble believing. A billion-dollar empire. Five national championships. Dinners with princes and friendships with kings. But none of that was the point. The point was the dream and the life it gave me.

If you have ever felt too old to start something new, this book is for you. If you have ever believed your background disqualifies you from success, this book is for you. If you have ever thought dreams are for other people, keep reading.

Through my story, you will discover three principles that turned an impossible dream into reality in my life: know your why, find your Velcro, and choose the right partners.

Your age does not matter. Your starting point does not matter. What matters is what you do next.

I once sat at the bottom of a pool ditch, wondering if that was all there was.

It was not. Not even close.

One

Profile of a Boy on His Way Up

I was three years old when I made my first great escape.

Our family spent the day at the Las Olas Casino Pool, an Olympic-size pool on the Atlantic Ocean. By late afternoon, everyone was sunburned and tired. One by one, my brother and my sisters climbed into my mother's Chevy Impala station wagon to head home. Doors slammed. The engine started.

That was when I noticed the window next to me was still down.

Through it, I could see the palm trees swaying against the late-afternoon sky and the last golden light skipping across the water. The whole world was still out there.

I pressed my small hands flat against the outside of the door, pulled myself up and over the window frame, and slid slowly down the warm metal until my bare feet touched the pavement. No one saw me. No one heard me. By the time my mother pulled out of the parking lot, I was already gone.

I was not trying to run away. I was not seeking attention. I was simply curious. Even at three, I wanted to see what else was out there, and this felt like my first chance to find out on my own.

A staff member at the pool spotted me wandering alone near the water and called the police. By six o'clock, I was live on the evening news across South Florida. A reporter looked into the camera and said, "Do you know this little boy in the green bathing suit? He knows his name is Tim, but he cannot remember where he lives."

At 1509 NE Sixth Street, the phone rang nonstop, and I was soon reunited with my family.

That night, my mother, determined to prevent any future adventures, created a system she believed was foolproof. She called it the "Dolly System." This system paired the three youngest siblings with the three older siblings, so the youngest kids had an older Dolly to keep an eye on them and help my mother.

This was my first lesson in teamwork. We looked after one another, supported one another when someone was down, and always made sure everyone was safe. We were stronger together than we could ever be alone. It was the only way our family could function. We continue to carry this system into our adult lives, always watching out for one another; we remain a team.

And in our house, that was just the beginning. Dinner was at six sharp. Study time was from seven to eight. Bedtime followed shortly after. The big kids had to make sure their Dolly had clean clothes, pack school lunches, and on Sundays, be appropriately dressed and

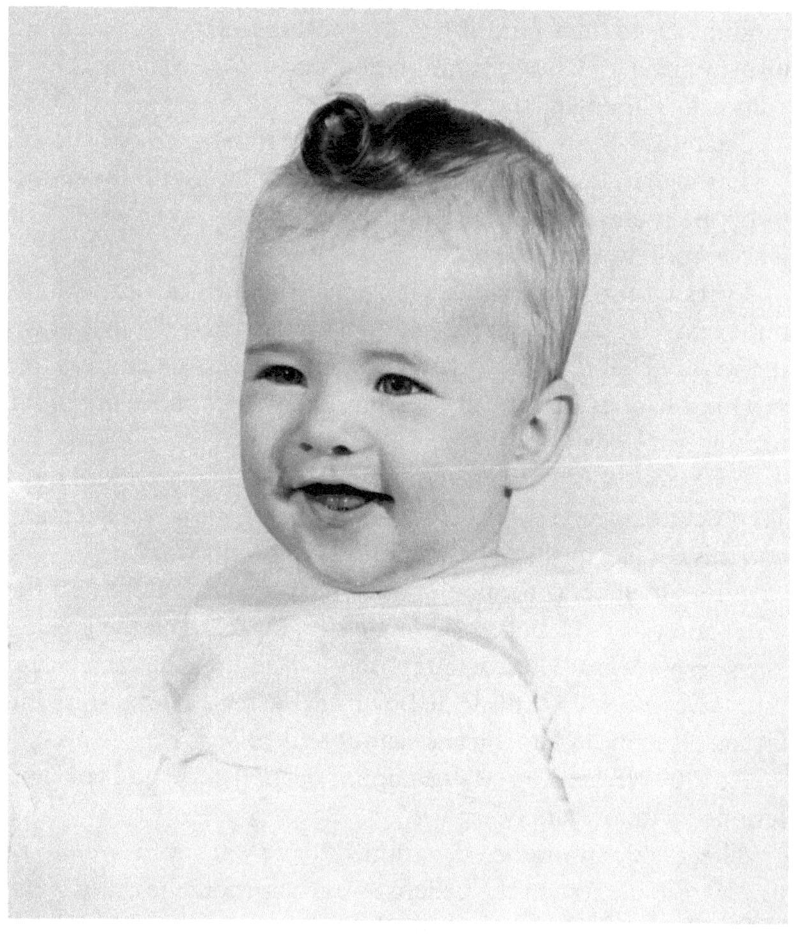

A young Adventurer, 1949.

ready for Mass.

By assigning these tasks, my mother could handle the rest of the household chores without constantly supervising her youngest children. No more being left at the pool. No more neighbors ringing the doorbell to say I was playing on the roof, where I enjoyed waving to everyone as they drove by. Yes, one day I figured out how to shimmy up the TV antenna pole onto the roof. I liked it up there; I could see more of what I might be missing. I was definitely a handful, a rambunctious, curious boy with endless energy. I was always looking for ways to stir up harmless fun or trouble. It did not matter which came first.

We lived in a three-bedroom, two-bathroom true Florida home with the nice, cool terrazzo floors for the hot summers. The three older sisters shared one room, my brother and I shared another, and my middle sister, Maureen (known as 'Mo' to the family), shared a third with my mother. Seven people under one small roof.

My family and I did everything together, the seven of us, our big, Irish, happy family. We went to the beach, swam, visited parks, and played games. I was young and did not feel deprived. I was just a small boy who knew he was loved by his mother and siblings. I rarely thought about not having a father in my life until one day in 3rd Grade.

Here I was in a small town full of rising stars. Fort Lauderdale was where future Chicago Bears star Brian Piccolo played Little League football at Holiday Park and where a young Chris Evert took tennis lessons from her father just down the road. On Sundays, we filled the pews at St. Anthony's alongside other large Catholic families. I cherished every aspect of my life, well, almost every aspect.

The image is still engraved in my memory: a small boy alone in the dugout, watching his teammates take the field from the shadows. I hear the crack of a bat, then see the ball arch toward our shortstop, followed by a clean throw to first base. Cheers erupt from the stands as my teammates slap gloves, while I remain stuck on the splintered bench, feeling the pain of exclusion deepen.

Without a father in the backyard to toss a ball with me, I was already behind the other boys. They had been throwing and catching for years. I was learning in the field, in front of everyone.

My coach was gentle, yet he kept me on the sidelines, allowing me to play only in the final merciful inning. When I finally had my shot, nerves overwhelmed me. Pop flies fell short before I could read their trajectory. Grounders skipped past my glove. Each mistake eroded my

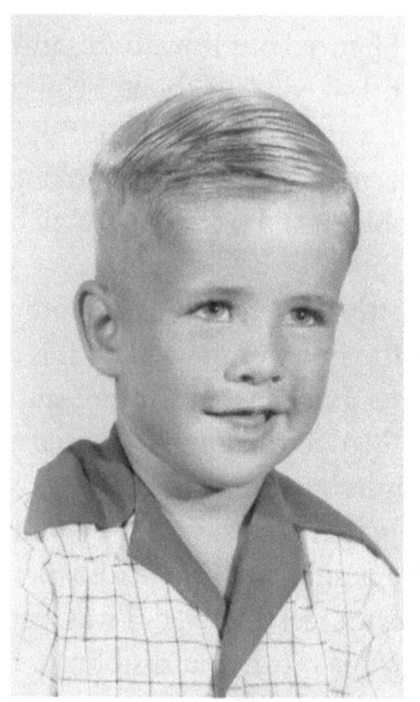

Childhood portrait. / The Gannon children. / The Gannon family, Fort Lauderdale, Florida

confidence and made my coach more reluctant to put me in again. At the plate, it was the same heartbreak: three rushed swings, three misses, and the long walk back to my bench.

Not having a father cost me more than baseball ever did. At St. Anthony's, the Catholic school run by the Adrian Dominican nuns, I was given a spelling test that required both parents' signatures. My father was not in my life, so I knew this would become a problem when I returned with only one parent's signature.

So the next day I returned to class with my mother's signature, and the teacher immediately asked, "Where is your father's signature?" I replied, "I don't have a father." She quickly became irritated and did not believe my story. I remember her name very vividly, Mrs. Thatcher, as she looked at me as if I had uttered the biggest lie. She said, "Everyone has a father!" and grew more agitated, asking, "Why would you lie to me?" I was maybe one of the five kids in the entire school living in a single-parent home.

The next thing I knew, she was dragging me down the hallway by my shirt to the principal's office. She explained what had happened. The principal listened carefully, then, in a sad, soft voice, said, "Listen, Mrs. Thatcher. John (my name at the time) doesn't have a father."

To this day, I still feel sorry for the guilt and embarrassment that the teacher went through once Sister Agnes explained to her that I really did not have a father. That is when I realized my life would be different. Not bad, but different.

After that moment, I remember deciding I needed to take more control over my life and my destiny. So the first thing I did was change my name from John Timothy Gannon to Tim Gannon. I disliked the name John; it sounded stiff and formal, so from that moment on, I was called Tim. It felt like I was making a fresh start for myself, on my own terms.

My mother was from Chicago, and her father, my grandfather, Howard Avery Brundage, whom I hold in great esteem, was also from Chicago. To the world, he was a prominent Chicago lawyer who represented George Halas, owner of the Chicago Bears; William Wrigley, of the chewing-gum empire and the Chicago Cubs; and John MacArthur, whose fortune now funds the MacArthur Genius Grants. He helped lead the Bears' players' union and drafted the first documents to protect professional athletes. In 1943, he became the first president of the Judge Advocates Association.

During the war, he served as an Army judge advocate. Afterward, he participated in the Nuremberg Trials, interrogating Nazi war criminals, including Hitler's Foreign Minister. A man of principle, he insisted that each German on trial have both an interpreter and a lawyer. He dedicated 10 years to those trials. It was a painful process that took a heavy toll on him.

But he never showed us pain. To us, he was simply Grandpa. I remember sitting on his knee as he made a quarter vanish from his palm, then pulled it out from behind my ear. His hands were steady, his voice calm. He taught me card tricks and coin tricks that I practiced for hours. I was convinced my grandfather had superpowers. As a young boy, I thought he glowed in the dark. He was my hero.

He was our main support in every way imaginable. He bought our house and cars. He visited us each year, and oh, how we loved seeing him. He would be so kind as to take us all to a nice, fancy restaurant, so we could taste a bit of the big life. My mother could not afford to take all 6 of us out, so it was a much-appreciated and special treat.

He would put us all on a train during the hot summer months and send us to the Smallbones Resort on Sisters Lake in Michigan. These visits and our trips together sparked my curiosity and a hunger to try something new.

In early 1961, when I was twelve, I lost my hero, my grandfather. While I did not fully grasp its significance at the time, his passing marked a turning point for me. He had been our stability, our safety net, and our link to a world far beyond our small Florida home on Sixth Street. He was the one who ensured we had a home, a car, and food on the table. He was the reason my sisters could attend college. He was the man who showed up when my father never did.

And now he was gone.

Soon after, my mother had to get a job as a social worker at Catholic Services and enrolled in a Master's program at Barry College in Miami. When she was not working, she was studying. She had a long, hard commute, so when she got home, she would just collapse in her chair from exhaustion. My Aunt Marie, who lived in a house behind our house, became ill and needed attention. My three older sisters were all in college or on their way to college by then, so my life as I once knew it was drifting apart, but I knew I had to do something to change it.

I was eager to earn money so I could make my own choices and stand on my own, so I took on my first job as a paper carrier boy, delivering for the Sun Sentinel. I started with 150 customers and quickly expanded my route to 300.

Shortly after that, I hired my first employee, who folded, banded, and bagged the papers, so all I had to do was deliver. Now that I had that part done, my next goal was to be even more efficient and time-effective, so I bought a Cushman Truckster and expanded my route to 900 customers, delivering to each in 2 hours. Eventually, the money I made from that tiny paper route, which started at 150 and grew to 900, allowed me to become more financially independent and achieve my short-term goals.

My success with my paper route earned me an article in the Fort Lauderdale News when I was 13. They named me Carrier of the Month. I still remember the pride I felt seeing my name in print. It was the first time I realized that if you worked harder than anyone else, people noticed. That paper route taught me more about business than any class ever could. I learned about customers, service, reliability, and the simple power of showing up every single day.

There I was, picture and all — "Profile of A Boy On His Way Up..." As the youngest of six kids, I have to say it felt good to receive recognition for my hard work and dedication, and to see how proud my mother was of me. I surely felt I was on my way up!

Later, that very paper route helped me buy my dream motorcycle, a Ducati 125, at age fourteen. Oh, she was a beautiful deep cranberry red. And she helped me deliver those 900 papers in record time. This Ducati also gave me the independence I had been dying for, the freedom to explore.

My mom always told us we had what it takes to succeed, good genes. I was not sure what that meant back then, but later in life, those good genes showed up and carried me through both the challenging and the good times.

But at fifteen, everything shifted. My mother put me on a bus to New Orleans to spend the summer with my father, a man I had never met. Nothing could have prepared me for what awaited me there.

PROFILE OF A BOY ON HIS WAY UP...

"Carrier of the Month"

At 13 years of age, John Timothy Ga
non is already a top-notch salesman.
course, he has many advantages — intere
in his work, a sense of responsibility to I
customers, and a friendly, polite personali
These traits are discernible by many su
scribers as well as the Fort Lauderdale Nev
Not one News subscriber on his downtov
Fort Lauderdale route has issued a con
plaint during his four months as a carrie

Tim (as he is known to everyone) lives
1509 N.E. 6th Street and attends St. A
thony's Church. The youngest member of t
Gannon family (4 sisters and 1 brother)
in the 8th grade at St. Anthony's Elementa
School. He belongs to the Study Club an
Math Club, and is the recipient of a perfe
attendance award. After graduation in Jun
he intends to join the student body of S
Thomas Aquinas High School.

Like many other youths his age, our Ca
rier-of-the-Month spends his leisure tim
playing baseball. He won a 2nd place pri
in his age group in a county eliminatic
tournament last year. He has chosen the A
Force as his favorite branch of service
Strategic Air Command if possible. I
proudly refers to an uncle, Captain Fai
child, who is with S.A.C. in Spokane, Was
ington.

Fort Lauderdale News Carrier of the Month.

Two

"What the Hell Did You Do to Get Down Here?"

At six every summer morning, I woke alone on the couch in my father's cramped, dim one-bedroom apartment, just as the first golden light crept across the New Orleans sky. But this summer was different; a clear turning point, where, in those quiet mornings, I sensed the subtle shift of my life transforming.

At fifteen, I wore my usual work outfit: blue jeans and a white T-shirt. I would pass the kitchen counter and small dining table, full of bottles, evidence of my father's bender the night before. After brushing my teeth, I headed out the door. By 6:15, I was on my way to my personal hell.

In our Fort Lauderdale home, his name was never even mentioned. He had left my mother and five siblings before I was born, which gave me no real reason to want to know him.

Curiosity always lingered. I wondered how he walked, the length of his stride, what his voice sounded like, and whether mine would match his. But honestly, these answers could have been found in just thirty seconds.

My mother believed I should spend two months with him before starting my sophomore year of high school. So she booked me a bus ticket in Florida and sent me to the Big Easy, where my dad was waiting at the station in the French Quarter. When he saw me, all he said was, "Let's go."

After 15 years of silence, the only words he spoke were those two. He stood before me, emotionally distant and hollow, a shell of someone I never knew. There was no hug, no sign of welcome.

For a moment, I searched his face for something, anything, a flicker of regret or a trace of curiosity about the son he had never known. There was nothing. Right there at the bus station, I realized this would be a long, painful summer.

He had run away from home at twelve and raised himself on the streets. No one had ever taught him how to be a father.

My father worked at Flamingo Pools as a clerk, ensuring supplies were delivered on time to job sites. My father thought it would be a good idea for me to work at the same company for those two months, so he secured a job for me in excavation and tying steel rebar. But the reality was more like a juvenile detention camp than a real job.

After leaving his apartment, I headed down lively Canal Street toward the trolley that stopped at every block. The city was coming alive around me, delivery trucks were busy restocking restaurants, the smell of fresh bread was drifting from bakeries, and street musicians were tuning up for the day. I stood in awe, soaking in the city's vibrant sights and energy.

Some mornings, I would stop at Café Du Monde for beignets and chocolate milk. The warm beignets melted on my tongue, their dusting of sugar sweetening my lips, while the rich, velvety chocolate milk washed everything down. During those brief moments, sitting there, I was not digging holes or confined to my father's apartment; I felt entirely at peace, and all my stress faded away.

Afterward, I boarded the trolley, which rattled and hummed as it stopped at every block. The familiar 'ding, ding, ding' of the bell still echoes in my memory. It carried me six miles to my destination each day.

During the forty-five-minute ride, I watched my fellow passengers, mostly Black men and women working as maids, laborers, and in other blue-collar jobs. I admired the determination etched in their faces, even during those early hours.

My gaze would then drift to the Garden District, where grand mansions with leaded glass windows and sparkling chandeliers lined St. Charles Avenue, homes to some of the South's wealthiest. I often imagined living in such a house, wondering about the daily lives inside, and wishing for a future like theirs.

It was then that my imagination began to wander beyond New Orleans, toward Europe, picturing the streets of Paris and London filled with Victorian and Neo-Gothic homes. I longed to go there someday, to discover the marvels and mysteries of cultures across the Atlantic.

After I reached my stop, I got off the trolley and walked half a mile to the job site. The work can be best described in three short words: hard as hell.

The heat was relentless. No breeze. No shade. Just 105 degrees pressing down like a weight. But no one knows heat like New Orleans in summer. It was the humidity that really got you. The air was so thick and wet it felt like breathing through a soaked blanket.

For eight hours a day, I either dug pool ditches or spent long periods tying steel rebar at the bottom. Tying rebar was even tougher than digging: it meant binding rods with four-inch wire, twisting them tightly by hand until they were secure. This process required hours of bending over beneath the harsh sun, causing aching backs, streaming sweat, and raw, wire-bitten hands. Every tie needed to be perfect, as the Gunite crew would later blast concrete to envelop the frame. Their job was the hardest, with rebar tying right behind, and neither was easy.

Normally, a chore for a fifteen-year-old kid is taking out the garbage. Doing this for eight hours seemed impossible. Having the day end seemed impossible.

Within minutes of working, my shirt was soaked, clinging to my back like a second skin. Sweat dripped into my eyes, stinging until I could barely see. My hands, raw from the wire, throbbed with every twist. Sometimes, an open sewer pipe would dump effluent directly into the pool we were building. We kept working.

I had never done manual labor in intense heat. It was an extraordinary experience, one that left me wondering: What the hell did I do to end up down here? What did I do wrong to be down in this hole?

Experiences like that burn into your memory so deeply that you remember them as clearly as if they happened yesterday. They embed themselves in your memory and never leave.

To this day, I do not like being in intense heat. I avoid that kind of intensity whenever I can.

I could not understand why my dad made me go through it. One would think that after never seeing me, he would show love and kindness. Instead, he was cold and distant.

I never brought lunch. Most of my coworkers were Black men, and when they realized I had no food, they shared their meals without hesitation. They did not have to. They barely knew me. Yet they handed me food and told me to eat as much as I wanted.

Their warmth caught me off guard. I had not spent much time around Black people before. It was the opposite of everything I knew from my father. These men, strangers in a pool ditch, showed me more kindness in a few weeks than my father had shown me in a lifetime. The outside world could be kinder than my own father.

Being backed into a corner often leads you to discover what you truly want from life. Difficult situations prompt you to reconsider your direction and hope for something better. I recall the days spent in sweat-soaked, muddy trenches, with no breeze for relief, and I could only envision a different future for myself.

My poor grades highlighted my lack of motivation; as I slept through most classes, I realized a change was necessary. That relentless, suffocating heat made me vow never to return to those trenches.

One day, during a break as we relaxed in the shade, one of the workers asked me, "What the hell did you do to get down here with us? You gotta go to college, young man. Your future isn't down here with us. Your future is out there in the world. We don't have a choice. We have to be in this goddamn ditch. But you have a choice. Get the hell out of here and make your own way in the world. Don't be like us."

These words struck a deep chord. I could not believe how kind these men were, but the fact that they saw something in me, a quality I could not see in myself, was a real aha moment. They gave me something my father never did: hope for a better future.

Several years later, I fell deeply in love with New Orleans. That city and everything it symbolized to me inspired the creation of what would become the most popular appetizer in history. Looking back, it all started with the kindness and love shown by those hardworking men in the ditches.

Three

The Flavor of New Orleans

That summer, two things from my father stuck with me. The crew did not respect him; they tolerated him, showing no affection, just as he showed me little. I was sure of one thing: I did not want to become like my father.

I also realized I was falling in love with New Orleans. Alone much of the time, I roamed the Crescent City's streets, drawn to live jazz and the scent of Creole food. My mother always said good Catholics go to heaven, but never mentioned New Orleans, which, to me, now felt like heaven on earth.

My deep craving for adventure was satisfied every time I stepped out of my father's miserable apartment and lost myself in the French Quarter, exploring restaurants, taste-testing foods, meeting eclectic people, and always stopping by Café Du Monde for beignets.

During those solo walks along the narrow streets, I felt a freedom I had never known. I realized for the first time that the world extended far beyond Fort Lauderdale, opening up to endless possibilities and excitement.

My love for New Orleans was a gift I gave myself, one that has stayed with me my whole life. My father never joined me on any of those trips. We never shared beignets or split a muffuletta. And surprisingly, that was the most meaningful gift he gave me: he showed me what I did not want to become.

The man had neither a family nor a future. He loved no one, and no one loved him. That is not who I wanted to be. The stark clarity of his empty life became a powerful influence on mine.

Looking back, my summer in New Orleans was a pivotal experience. After two months of tough work in 105degree heat, pounding a shovel into the dirt for Flamingo Pools, I realized one thing for sure: I never wanted to dig pools for a living.

Up to this point, I had been a C- student. I never really tried in school and was not interested in hitting the books, unlike my three oldest sisters, who all earned straight A's. Now, after the eye-opening events of my summer in New Orleans, I realized I needed a plan. I knew I would not achieve anything in life if I did not start taking school more seriously.

So when I returned home, I put more effort into my studies. My mother was completely uninvolved in my schooling; as long as I did not fail out, she overlooked my grades. Before eleventh grade, just days after I returned, I asked her if I could transfer from Catholic school to a public one.

Why did I want to leave St. Thomas Aquinas? It was run by Dominican nuns and had approximately 1,000 students. But I wanted a break from the rigors and rigidness of Catholic school, a breather from uniforms, endless rules, and the harshness of the nuns.

My brother Pete and I were in the same grade, and we both wanted a break from that routine to see what the other side was like. Put simply, I just wanted to be a normal kid in a public school. My mom agreed; Pete and I enrolled at Fort Lauderdale High at the start of our junior year.

Around this time, my brother Pete and I took on a second job: parking cars at The Mai-Kai.

The Mai-Kai was founded by brothers Jack and Bob Thornton, who had served in the Pacific during World War II. From the parking lot, I could hear the drums and the music from the shows inside. Tiki torches lined the entrance, casting flickering light on giant wooden sculptures. The thatched roof rose above lush tropical gardens, and through the windows I caught glimpses of the dancers in their feathered costumes.

It was another world, and I stood at its edge, waiting for the next set of keys.

What I remember most is how the Thorntons treated people. They were true gentlemen who respected their guests and employees alike. That lesson in leadership has stayed with me.

I never imagined this industry would become my career. All I knew was that Joe DiMaggio, Jack Nicklaus, Johnny Carson, and Hugh Downs dined at The Mai-Kai, where I parked their cars for $1.15 an hour.

Very few teenagers had the chance to sit behind the wheel of a 1966 Jaguar XKE convertible or a James Bond-style Aston Martin. But I was one of them. As I slid into those leather seats, a sense of pure adventure washed over me. I pictured myself cruising along the Riviera, a moment that sparked my love for classic cars.

Initially, I noticed little change in my life. Setting intentions was simple, but forming habits proved difficult. My mind was foggy, like being in a cloud. Although my grades improved due to the renewed motivation I gained in New Orleans, I continued to sleep through classes, deliver newspapers after school, and park cars at night.

Having two jobs left me no time for homework and drained my energy to focus. This cycle felt endless, like a personal Dark Age. Not belonging to any school team or club made me invisible to teachers and classmates alike. I had made a vow in that New Orleans ditch, but back in Florida, the vow felt distant, like something I had said to myself in a dream.

Then, everything shifted. It was the second semester of my junior year, classes already underway, when a new student walked into my Algebra II class.

Four

A Friend Who Changed Everything

As the train carried me back to Fort Lauderdale a few weeks before my junior year, I was certain of two things: I never wanted to dig another ditch, and I never wanted to become my father. I was not thinking about college. I had no real plan, only a restless desire to see more of the world.

My life was small. I was delivering newspapers in the afternoon, parking cars at The Mai-Kai restaurant at night, and getting through school each day. That was it. But with the start of the new school year, something shifted. In my Algebra II class, I struck up a conversation with another student.

We sat in alphabetical order, with my last name beginning with G and his with H: Phil Heatley. One day, feeling bored, we whispered to each other to avoid catching the teacher's attention. I confessed I was not interested in Algebra; I preferred understanding the world. I will never forget Phil's response to this.

"There's a world out there called polo," he said. "My father played it. He now raises horses in El Paso, Texas."

Phil leaned closer, energized. "My father sells horses to wealthy clients in New York and Chicago, mostly polo players. He finds ex-racehorses in El Paso and trains them as polo ponies. Why don't you come out there? You could help train them and come along when we show them to buyers."

"Wow," I said. "That sounds like a great job."

Phil grinned. "Have you ever ridden a horse before? Or exercised one?"

"No, no, and no," I said quickly. "I've never even seen a horse in real life before."

"Well, that's about to change," Phil said with a knowing smile.

I was fifteen. My adventure was about to begin.

Just days after our conversation in Algebra class, Phil took me to a polo match in Boca Raton.

Years later, Phil looked back on that moment. "I was a military brat, but by the time Tim and I met, my father had mostly finished his career and retired in El Paso. He married a woman who owned a farm. He bought land next to it, and the two properties merged. His business became raising thoroughbred racehorses. When I mentioned polo, Tim was immediately intrigued. We just clicked. From that day on, we were best friends. We still are."

From the moment I saw the horses, the riders, and the speed and fury of the play, I was hooked. There was no other word for it.

What makes polo so irresistible? Phil explained it in a way I have not forgotten. "It is this feeling that you are on a thousand-pound animal, a horse, and you have got to guide it," he said. "That is just the start. Then you have all the demands of swinging a mallet and hitting a ball on the ground while you are eight feet in the air. You are doing this as the horse gallops at full speed. It is not easy. But when you connect with the ball, there is an immediate gratification."

Phil and I found a spot near the sideboards, close enough to feel the ground tremble.

The field stretched endlessly in front of us, incredibly vast. Phil mentioned it was the length of three football fields. The goalposts at each end, white and set against the green turf, were twenty-four feet apart. This was no casual backyard game. The Orthweins, heirs to the Anheuser-Busch brewing fortune and among America's wealthiest families, were playing. The Busch family was also present. This was high-goal polo, the real thing.

A horn sounded. The first chukker began.

"Each period is seven and a half minutes," Phil said, leaning close so I could hear him over the thunder of hooves. He mentioned that these periods are called chukkers, with most games consisting of six. After seven minutes, a horn sounds, signaling that thirty seconds remain.

The horses rushed past us so closely that I could feel the wind from their bodies. They were moving at around thirty-five miles an hour, maybe even faster. The speed was breathtaking. One rider kept the ball airborne with his mallet, then swung and hit it before it touched the ground. The crack echoed across the field.

I watched a rider in a white jersey drive downfield, his mallet a blur. He struck the ball cleanly, and it sailed between the posts.

"Goal," Phil said. "Now watch. They switch sides."

"Every time someone scores?"

"Every time. Keeps it fair if the wind or sun favors one end."

The teams reversed. I noticed the players wore numbers on their jerseys: one through four.

Phil explained, "The number indicates a player's position. Position one is the scorer, similar to a striker in soccer. Position four is the last line of defense, as polo has no goalies. Positions two and three are the workhorses, with three serving as the playmaker. He's like the quarterback, often the captain, and typically the top-rated player on the field."

A collision near midfield made me flinch. Two horses slammed into each other, shoulder to shoulder, and one pushed the other sideways without breaking stride. The impact's sound carried across the field.

"That's a bump," Phil said. "The horses are trained to handle it. Push another horse over at thirty-five miles an hour and keep going. It takes years to teach them. It's legal as long as the angle isn't too steep, forty-five degrees or less."

A whistle blew. One of the umpires raised his hand.

"Foul," Phil said. "He crossed the line of the ball. That's the most important rule. When the ball is hit, it creates an imaginary line. Whoever is on that line has the right-of-way. You can't just cut in front of them. Dangerous for the horses."

The fouled team took a penalty shot. The ball rocketed into the goal.

"About forty percent of all points come from penalties," Phil said. "That's why positioning matters more than power."

At halftime, something unexpected happened. Spectators began walking onto the field.

"Divot stomp," Phil grinned. "The horses tear up the turf. Everyone helps press the divots back down. Come on."

We entered the field together, I felt the soft grass give under my feet. The smell hit me first: cut grass, horse sweat, and something sweeter drifting from the champagne flutes the women carried. Nearby, men in blazers and women in sundresses were stomping the earth flat, sipping drinks, chatting, and laughing.

The players had dismounted to exchange horses. Up close, the horses shimmered with sweat, their muscles rippling beneath their coats. I pressed a chunk of torn turf back into the earth with the sole of my sneaker and thought: I want to be on the other side of these sideboards.

It was graceful. It was ballet. It was battle and beauty wrapped together.

I had never been part of anything like this. A sport where the crowd becomes part of the game. Where wealth and tradition mixed with mud and muscle.

For more than an hour, I could not take my eyes off the field. The daring of the riders. The swing of the mallets. The grace of the galloping horses. The joy on a player's face when his team scored.

I did not want to leave. I wanted to live inside this world forever.

I had never played team sports as a young child. I did not have a father to teach me, practice with me, or guide me. But watching this match, I believed I had found a sport where I could one day belong.

The only issue was the cost. Polo horses are very expensive; a prime, well-trained pony can cost over $50,000, and multiple horses are required. Each horse may play only one chukker before being switched. Top players own or lease up to ten horses, and lessons cost between $1,000 and $1,500. For a child without money, playing polo seemed impossible.

But in those ditches in New Orleans, I had made a decision. My circumstances would not dictate my future. Now, watching these riders, I finally knew what that future looked like. I did not know how I would get there. I only knew I would.

After that first match, I helped Phil land a job parking cars alongside me. We soon realized how much we had in common. However, there was one major difference: Phil had great admiration for his father. I had none for mine. Because Phil's father lived far away, they met only during the summers.

Like me, Phil was raised by his mother. We both longed for guidance from men we could look up to. That longing explained my eagerness to meet Phil's father, a disciplined military man Phil described as one of the most remarkable people he had ever known.

Our trip to El Paso at the end of the school year could not come soon enough.

Phil recalled, "I knew Tim would thrive at the ranch because he was such a hard worker. He'd handle a massive paper route, then go straight to parking cars well past midnight. Tim and his brother Pete always closed the restaurant, often staying until two or three in the morning. I left at midnight because my mother insisted I'd be too tired for school otherwise. She was right. During class, Tim would be dozing off from all those late nights. But seeing his work ethic, I knew my dad was going to love him."

I counted the days until we left town and headed west. It would be my first great adventure, and it would change me in ways I could not have imagined.

Five

The Journey to El Paso

Four words set everything in motion: "Let's go to El Paso."

That was what Phil Heatley told me a few weeks after we met in Algebra II class during my junior year at Fort Lauderdale High School. Phil shared his plan: we would stay at the horse ranch his father owned, spending our days working and riding, then retiring at night to a tack room converted into a bedroom with a bath and shower.

Phil emphasized that his father, a seasoned military man who had served in the Army Corps of Engineers in Europe during World War II, was a strict taskmaster who demanded 100% effort every day. But I assured him I knew what hard work looked and felt like; I thought nothing could be more exhausting than digging pool ditches in New Orleans during the 105-degree summer heat.

Up to this point, my life had mostly involved selling newspapers, parking cars, struggling with sports, and getting by academically. I had not done anything truly remarkable, and no one, aside from my family, would notice if I disappeared.

Using money I earned from my newspaper route and parking cars at The MaiKai, I bought a 1957 Chevy convertible for $600 in cash, a small fortune for a teenager in the 1960s and a big upgrade from the Cushman Truckster my brother and I drove on our paper route. My brother Pete called it "the cat's meow." It was a dream car, a collector's item, a turquoise blue convertible.

I will never forget the feeling that washed over me as I handed the man the cash for the Chevy: it was as if everything was about to begin. This transaction meant I was all-in. There was no turning back now, even though that thought never crossed my mind. The sense of freedom that rushed through me as I slid behind the wheel for the first time was exhilarating, as intoxicating as anything I had ever experienced. All that lay in front of me was a ribbon of road, and it was beautiful. For the first time, I was the captain of my own ship and my own life.

The day after school ended for the summer, Phil, his brother Johnny, and I threw our bags into the trunk of the Chevy and sped off from Fort Lauderdale to start our great summer adventure. As we drove beyond the city limits and the tall buildings faded from my rearview mirror, we felt energized, hopeful, and full of wonder, just like teenagers. Mile after mile, with the top down, we watched the lush Florida land rush by as we traveled north along the coast, three teenage boys with the wind in their hair and without a care in the world.

Everything was as we had pictured it until we heard a big boom. Smoke started to billow from under the hood. The engine sputtered. Uh oh.

I drove the Chevy, huffing and puffing, to a service station in Vero Beach. The mechanic's news was not good: the engine had failed and needed replacing. "It's not cheap," the owner told us. "But if you help me, I'll get you back on the road." Phil, Johnny, and I exchanged puzzled looks. None of us knew a thing about engines or how to rebuild one.

We had two options. One, we could have called home and sent a distress signal to our parents, explaining the situation and asking them to wire money. But we barely had enough cash for hotels and food; we certainly did not have enough for parts and labor. I could have told my mother, "Hey, we're in Vero Beach, and we are stuck." But I knew her answer: "Come back home now!" That was not an option. I was not going to let my first real adventure end after one hundred miles.

Option two: The local station owner offered to help us, but he said, "As a team, we rebuild the engine together." Without hesitation, we decided we would be thrilled to help!

Over the next twenty-four hours, the owner patiently guided us through each step, offering clear instructions. We regarded him as our teacher, and, like eager students, we absorbed every word as though it echoed down from the heavens. In many ways, he was our guardian angel. He could have easily charged us $700 for his help, but instead, he asked for payment only for the parts.

We started work with focused determination, noses under the hood, hands coated with grease, doing precisely as instructed. It was a true education in automotive mechanics. Under his careful eye, we ground valves and bored cylinders. Even as the sun set, we kept going. All night, beneath the glittering South Florida stars, we pushed on. At dawn, with the first light over the Atlantic, we remained undeterred. Finally, by afternoon, every component perfectly reassembled, I took the driver's seat, turned the key, and my '57 Chevy convertible roared to life. I had never heard a sweeter sound.

The three of us hugged each other and then embraced the station owner as if he were our father. Once again, I realized that the real world can be kinder and more generous than I expected. We paid him for his help and then drove out of the station and back onto the highway.

We believed nothing could stop us from reaching El Paso now.

Our money was gone, every last cent spent on the rebuilt engine. The only thing we could rely on was the Phillips 66 credit card my mom had given me. We could fill the Chevy's gas tank, but that was about it. Back then, in the summer of 1966, service stations were scarce.

You could not buy a pizza, a taco, a hot dog, a cappuccino, or a Frappuccino at nearly every gas station, as you can today. In those days, a Phillips 66 station offered gas and maybe a few candy bars. That is what we survived on as we drove 1,910 miles, roughly twenty-seven hours, to El Paso.

We definitely did not have money for a motel room, not even for one of those seedy places where you often leave with an itch.

The first night after leaving Vero Beach, after about ten hours on the road, we pulled over at what we thought was a deep lake. Still greasy from rebuilding the engine, we needed to clean up. After stopping, we dug through our bags and quickly realized another problem: none of us had any soap. But the thing about adventures, and life and business, is that you always have to adapt. Instead of soap, we grabbed a can of shaving cream and decided it would be our way of cleaning.

We stripped down to our underwear and covered ourselves with white shaving cream. Looking like three miserable snowmen, we trudged into the muddy lake waters. Unfortunately, it was only six inches deep. We tried splashing ourselves with the dirty water to wash away the dirt and grime, but all we washed away was the shaving cream. By the time we came out, we were still coated in grease. Seeing how silly we looked, we laughed so hard we doubled over.

That is another key to succeeding in life: if you can laugh at yourself, you can handle almost anything.

As songs blared from the radio, including "Lil' Red Riding Hood" by Sam the Sham & The Pharaohs and "You Can't Hurry Love" by the Supremes, we kept rolling along, hugging the Gulf Coast as we passed through Alabama, Mississippi, and Louisiana. We crossed into Texas and drove the entire Lone Star State from east to west before finally arriving in El Paso, a border town in the far western corner of Texas that touches both New Mexico and Mexico.

Exhausted yet excited, we finally arrived at Twin Farms ranch, our long journey at an end. Stepping out of my convertible, I surveyed the landscape: flat as an ironing board, with tumbleweeds rolling across the open terrain. There were likely more trees on my block back in Fort Lauderdale than within miles of this place.

Even though no one would have believed me, I genuinely thought I had just found my paradise, my Eden. For the first time in my life, I felt as if I had stepped out of the darkness and into something that mattered.

It was during this period of newfound clarity and hope that I met Phil's dad, Bud Heatley. Most intriguing about Bud was this: he was a polo player. I had never met anyone in person who had played polo, and I hung on his every word when he described what it was like to play at Squadron A Armory in New York City and at world-renowned venues like Meadowbrook on Long Island.

This man had led a full, exciting, and invigorating life, and that was what I aspired to for myself. He was the first to introduce the idea of escapism into my thoughts, that you can always change the direction of your life if you have the will to take chances and a strong belief in yourself.

Bud stayed remarkably active well into his sixties. He frequently traveled along the East Coast to attend polo matches, always enthusiastically hoping to sire a Kentucky Derby contender with his prized stallion, Carbonated. With dozens of horses in training at Twin Farms, Bud quickly found work for Phil, Phil's brothers, Jeff,

Johnny, and me.

"My dad had been involved with horses his entire life, even when he was in the military," Phil said. "He was a very accomplished jump rider for open jumping. His real passion in life was entirely horses. And I think some of that rubbed off on Tim. My dad had a real outgoing personality and a tremendous love of life and horses. Tim came to realize that life had meaning, and that was why he was driven to succeed."

Six

Phil's Dad: A Man's Man

As soon as we arrived at Twin Farms, Bud Heatley walked toward us with an unyielding posture that spoke volumes, the straightness of his back a reflection of the strength and discipline that defined him.

Phil had already told me all about his father. Bud embodied the qualities I admired most: a man who had explored the world, lived boldly, and served with distinction. A veteran of the Army Corps of Engineers in World War II, Bud had re-enlisted out of patriotism when the Korean War broke out, once again joining the Corps. His military service took him far and wide, and he seemed to know people everywhere.

The military had shaped him. His boots were always perfectly shined, everything in order. Yet he was no stiff officer. Bud had the charm of an Irishman and could tell stories that held you captive for hours. He was one of the most charming people I had ever met.

But Bud's prowess as a horseman inspired me most. Whether training Thoroughbreds for racing, schooling green horses into skilled polo ponies, or jumping at top venues like Madison Square Garden and challenging Long Island courses, he excelled at it all. Polo was in his blood. His father had played, and his grandfather before him had played.

After WWII, Bud competed across Europe aboard a remarkable horse named Gavilon, owned by Prince Bernhard of the Netherlands. Watching Bud in the saddle was striking. Before long, I began to see him as a father figure.

Bud's first job for us was something straight out of Mark Twain's *The Adventures of Tom Sawyer*, painting all fifty horses' stalls by hand. He handed each of us a brush and some paint and told us to get to work. After two hours, we realized that at this pace, it would take days, if not weeks, to complete. We acted quickly and borrowed a paint sprayer from a nearby rancher, completing the project in one day. That was a win for the boys! Let us just say that is when we learned the skill of working smarter, not harder.

Bud Heatley addressing his troops during World War Two.

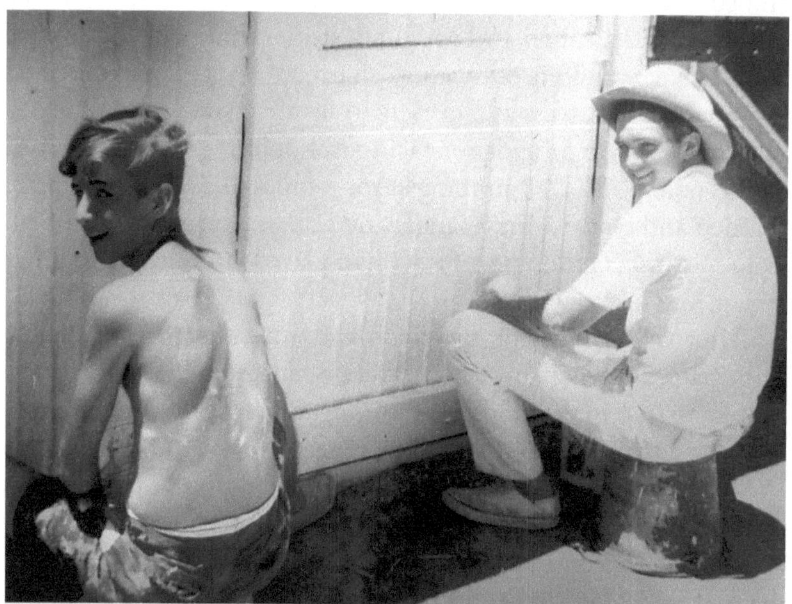

Painting Bud Heatley's stables in El Paso with Phil.

"My dad was really upset about us using a spray gun," Phil said. "He had planned for us to paint the stalls by hand all summer. He was trying to teach us what it meant to work hard. But he definitely found other ways to get us to work."

Bud gave each of us a shovel and assigned us the task of transporting a huge pile of horse manure to a distant spot. We spent three exhausting weeks shoveling it without taking any shortcuts.

I remember one day in particular. The sun was barely up, but the heat was already pressing down. By mid-morning, my shirt was soaked through. The smell of manure filled my nostrils, and my hands were raw from gripping the shovel. My back ached. My arms burned. Sweat dripped into my eyes.

Although it was tough, I did not mind putting in the time.

Having friends by my side made the work feel like an adventure, bringing to mind digging ditches in New Orleans, but this time, the great company of good friends made all the difference.

"My father was very demanding about work," Phil said. "Tim's introduction to the horse world wasn't easy, with the manure relocation that took about three weeks to finish. It was a rough life. There was a bunkhouse. In the barn attached to the stables, there was a tack room and a small room next to it where Tim and I stayed. It had a bathroom and two cots. That's where we slept and lived. Connected to that were the stables with about seventy stalls for the racehorses. There was no air conditioning, and it was hot as hell in the summer. To me, it was not very pleasant."

But it was for me. For six weeks, we worked hard under the blazing Texas sun, completing the tasks Bud assigned us. But in the evenings, from time to time, we got to relax a little.

A couple of times, we jumped into my convertible and crossed the Rio Grande into Mexico, heading for Juarez. We were sixteen, exploring a border town, and having the time of our lives. For the first time, I felt truly free.

Other times, we saddled up some of Bud's Thoroughbreds and hit the trail. I had never ridden a horse before, so it took me some time to learn to control it. One evening, the boys played a prank on me. They rigged the bit so that it fell out of my horse's mouth as soon as we started riding. When this happened, the horse took off, running out of control. I held on for dear life, bouncing up and

With Johnny, Phil, and Jeff Heatley on the manure pile at Twin Farms.

down on the horse, but finally I got him under control. I was scared to death, but I loved it!

"Tim was game for anything," Phil said. "He totally embraced all of that. You could see he wanted to be part of the horse world."

Galloping along the Rio Grande as it flowed through the desert were the best moments of my life so far. The Texas twilight made me feel free as I rode, guiding my Thoroughbred along the winding riverbank. Every worry faded during those rides; only the joy of the moment mattered, and I let it fill my soul. Something had taken hold of me, not just Thoroughbreds and riding, but the idea of polo itself, even though I had never swung a mallet.

One afternoon, I confided in Bud my dream of becoming a polo player. We sat down after a hard day's work as the sun dropped behind the mountains, turning the sky a deep copper. The horses had settled for the evening, and I could hear them shifting in the barn behind us, the soft thud of hooves on packed dirt. Even though I was just a teenager with no experience or resources, Bud did not laugh or dismiss my ambitions. Instead, he offered advice that would stay with me forever.

"Son, it takes a lot of money to become a professional polo player," he said.

"How do I make a lot of money?" I asked, revealing just how young and green I was.

"There are three ways to make a lot of money," Bud said. "The first is to go out and marry a rich woman. That's the hard way. You have to love that woman and behave. The second way is to get an excellent education. You've got to go to Harvard or Yale and then get offered a position with a blue-chip firm on Wall Street or in finance. And the third way is to bring something to the marketplace."

At sixteen, I never considered the first option; I had no idea how to find and marry a wealthy woman. The second option was just as confusing. I had slept through much of school, so my grades were not good enough for the Ivy League, and I had zero interest in college. That left only the third and final choice as a viable path.

I asked Bud what he meant by "bringing something to the marketplace," and he asked if I knew who George De Mestral was. I did not. Bud then took a deep breath and told me the story of the brilliant Swiss inventor. Class was in session.

It went like this: George De Mestral loved the outdoors. He was an engineer by training, and his specialty was agronomy, which Bud explained was the science of soil management and crop production. In simple terms, it dealt with crops, soil, and farm machinery. One day in the early 1940s, De Mestral returned from a day in the field to find his pants and his dog covered in burrs. As he pulled the burrs off his dog's coat, he became increasingly curious. How did they attach themselves so tightly? What mechanism allowed them to cling so easily yet proved so tricky to remove?

De Mestral had access to a machine shop at his company. As an agronomist, he was trained to analyze and inspect a wide range of items. When he examined a burr under a microscope, he realized that each of its teeth was actually a hook that latched onto the fibers of his clothing and the hairs of his dog's coat. This discovery fascinated him. And so began his decade-long pursuit to create the hook-and-loop fastener now known as "Velcro."

"Why didn't somebody else invent Velcro?" I asked Bud.

"Think about it," Bud replied. "How many of us have the training to analyze something as microscopic as a burr the way De Mestral did? Or the tools he had at his disposal, the small, delicate instruments that could surgically put a tiny loop together with a hook?

And what about the patience and persistence that Velcro required? How many of your friends would be willing to spend a decade on an idea that may or may not even have any marketable value?"

Following De Mestral's invention of Velcro, the market's enthusiastic response took even him by surprise. NASA quickly adopted Velcro for its space suits, preferring it over traditional zippers or buttons. Have you ever seen those on a space suit? Velcro's versatility made it the perfect choice, not just for gloves and pants, but also for skier's parkas. Before long, the entire outdoor industry had adopted Velcro as well.

The market for De Mestral's hook-and-loop fastener grew so large that today the Velcro Companies produce over 35,000 products. And that was Bud's point.

"If you want to play polo, you have to find your Velcro," he told me. "It's as simple as that, Tim. Find your Velcro."

For days on the ranch, his words echoed in my mind, on dusty trails, in the dim stables, and during quiet moments before sunrise. I kept wondering what my own 'Velcro' might be and what it would take to realize my dreams.

Finally, I went back to Phil with a concrete plan. "Here's the deal," I said. "Whoever ends up making it big and earning the most will pay for our polo team, and the other will manage it."

He held out his hand and took mine. "Deal," he said.

This was a significant victory for me because deep down, I believed Phil was destined for greatness. Everyone liked Phil. He was intelligent, sharp, well-presented, and loved by teachers and classmates. As for me? I was painfully shy, an unremarkable student, socially awkward, and mostly invisible. Yet, I had one thing in abundance: determination. I knew I wanted to be a polo player. That became my primary goal in life. Bud Heatley gave me a clear roadmap for achieving it.

"Son, it won't be easy," he told me.

"I don't care if it's easy or not," I said. "I'm going to do it. Somehow, some way, I'm going to do it."

Bud knew I was facing impossible odds, but he did something I will never forget: he believed in me. He could have belittled me and said I was wasting my time chasing a wild dream. Instead, he encouraged me.

At the end of our stay, as we were getting ready to leave Twin Farms and head back to Florida, Bud walked out to my '57 Chevy carrying a polo saddle, it was a Stalker Nafey. He handed it to me and said, "Put it to good use."

I stood there, holding the saddle in my arms. The leather was worn and smooth from years of use. It smelled of horses, sweat, and hard work. I did not know what to say.

I did not have a horse. Even if I had one, I would not know how to ride it well enough to play polo. But that was not Bud's point. With this gesture, he was encouraging me to chase my dreams. He was challenging me to live a bolder life, to become an adventurer, to take risks, and to saddle up.

I still vividly remember driving away from the ranch all those years ago, looking over my shoulder and seeing Bud smile and wave.

Driving home with the top down, we cruised through the expansive Texas flatlands. The warm summer wind played across my cheeks, and in that moment, it felt like my life was just about to begin.

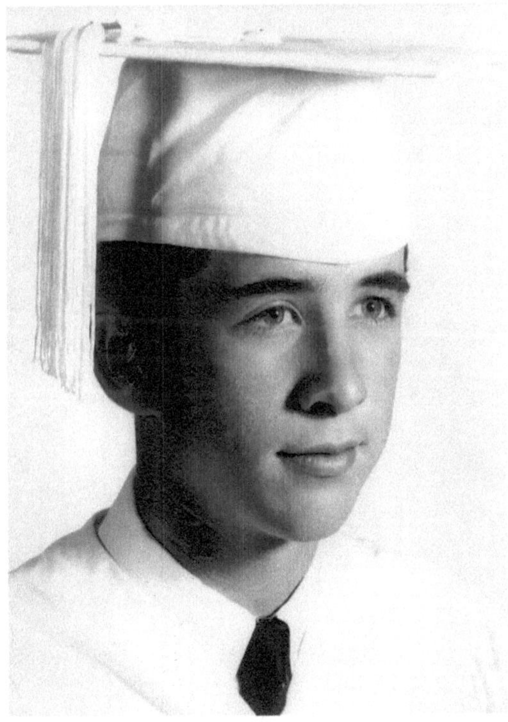

High school graduation

Seven

The Adventures Begin

I could not get polo out of my mind. Driving my '57 Chevy away from the ranch and along the rural dirt roads, kicking up a trail of dust behind me, I kept replaying my conversations with Bud Heatley. I was already obsessed with the sport and determined to see it played at the highest level, to understand what kind of skill it would take for me to succeed one day.

Even before we left Twin Farms, I had a plan. Instead of going back to Fort Lauderdale, we would head to New York City to see the sights and sounds of the world's most energetic city, then go to Long Island to watch professional polo matches. After some persuasion, my three partners in crime agreed to my spontaneous idea.

What a foursome we were, Phil, his brothers Jeff and Johnny, and I, as we cruised across Texas with the top down on the Chevy, the sun shining, the wind blowing, and our dreams running wild. For the first time in my life, I had a clear plan: I would go to college (even though my grades were terrible), I would find a way to become successful (or Phil would), and then Phil and I would become professional polo players. To my sixteen-year-old mind, it all sounded so simple.

I realized my job in Fort Lauderdale would take me nowhere. If I kept parking cars at The Mai-Kai, maybe one day I would be promoted to manage the valet stand full-time, like Butch Dewar, who had spent forty years running the parking operation for the Thorntons. Or maybe my paper route at the Sun Sentinel could turn into something more, perhaps even a job in the printing plant. Those options had once seemed appealing, at least until my aha moment at Twin Farms with Bud Heatley. After that, I knew I had to find a way to get into college.

But first, we had one more adventure to undertake in the summer of 1966. We drove to St. Louis, where we dropped off Phil for his new job. Using his father's connections, Phil got a job grooming for one of polo's top players, Ray Harrington. After saying goodbye to Phil and telling him we would meet up in a few weeks back in Florida, I climbed back into the Chevy with Jeff and Johnny, heading to the Big Apple.

A deep transformation was happening inside me. Before my time at Twin Farms, I was an introverted, shy, and awkward sixteen-year-old boy who had rarely traveled more than a hundred miles from Fort Lauderdale, until my car broke down. If Phil had not been with me, I probably would have called home for help. Instead, with his encouragement, we kept going as a team, fixed the engine, and turned the setback into a great adventure.

Now, I did not want that adventure to end, even though the person who had left Fort Lauderdale two months earlier no longer existed. I felt confident, assured, and self-reliant. I was ready to chase my dreams, no matter how much effort they required.

We reached the outskirts of Manhattan, where the skyscrapers in the distance seemed to reach up and touch the sky. I drove through the Lincoln Tunnel, the longest tunnel I had ever been in, and then we emerged into the bustling heart of the city: Times Square. We parked and strolled through the city, exploring and watching people from all over the world gather in the City That Never Sleeps. To a teenager who had never been to New York, this was an eye-opening, breathtaking experience.

Seeing Wall Street, Broadway, Central Park, the grand museums, Rockefeller Center, and the Statue of Liberty reaffirmed how vast the world was. More than ever, the frontiers of possibility expanded for me as I walked the streets, feeling the energy and excitement that was palpable with every step.

After a few days in the Big Apple, we packed into my Chevy and headed east along the Long Island Expressway to reach Long Island, home to some of the most renowned polo clubs in the country. If I were going to become a polo player, I needed to see the game firsthand.

The Heatley family owned a house in the Hamptons, a place where the rich and famous hobnob. After we dropped off our bags, we headed straight to a polo club, hoping to catch a match.

Then we saw it: professional players galloping around the field.

I had seen polo played by amateurs in Fort Lauderdale, but this was on a different level, like attending an NFL game instead of a high school contest.

The skill was incredible, the way they aggressively chased the ball and swung their mallets with uncanny accuracy. I loved everything about it and, deep down, believed this was what I wanted to do in the future. Somehow, some way, I was going to become a professional polo player.

That experience lingered as I returned to everyday life. At home, I talked with Phil and told him I would be attending Broward County Junior College, where tuition was only a few hundred dollars per semester. After working hard in the classroom at BCJC, I told Phil we would attend Florida State together in our sophomore year. He liked the idea.

As high school graduation approached, Phil devised another plan. Once school was over, he would go to the ranch in El Paso, load twelve horses onto a hauler, and drive them first to Chicago, then up to upstate New York. When I mentioned that I had family in Chicago, he said he would pick me up there, along with another friend from Fort Lauderdale, Nick Copalis. From there, the three of us would continue our trip to the Empire State. I could hardly wait.

But just a few days before he was scheduled to leave Texas, Phil took a nasty fall off a horse and hurt his back. The injury was so severe that he could not drive or make the trip. Waiting for him with Nick at a cheap hotel outside Chicago, we finally heard that Phil would not be coming. At that point, Nick and I needed to regroup. We spent that first night riding the "L" train in a loop, discussing potential options. Finally, I suggested visiting my grandmother, who lived at the Edgewater Beach Hotel in downtown Chicago, but by then, my grandfather had passed away. "I can borrow some money," I told Nick, "so we'll have enough cash to take a Trailways bus home." At that moment, I did not even have ten dollars in my wallet. Everything I did was on a shoestring budget.

Nick and I went to my grandmother's fancy place at Edgewater. She came from a wealthy family, with limousines, chauffeurs, cooks, and the whole luxury package. As we stepped into her large apartment, the first thing I noticed was the sparkling diamond earrings she was wearing. I did not know her well; she only visited us in Fort

Lauderdale from time to time. Almost as soon as we arrived, she looked at us and asked, "Oh, what are you doing here?"

"I was going to work for a friend named Phil," I said. "But he's been in an accident, and now he can't come." She shot me a puzzled look. She had no idea who Phil was, and frankly, she barely knew who I was or anything about my life.

After a few moments of awkward silence, I said, "Grandma, I need about forty dollars to get home." Suddenly, she began to shake visibly. I could not believe it. Here I was, a seventeen-year-old, looking at his grandmother, surrounded by wealth, and she was trembling over a request for forty dollars.

"I knew you were coming here to get money from me," she said sternly, looking me in the eyes.

I immediately thought: Holy shit, I'm going to get in trouble for this. So I dropped the subject. "Never mind, I'm good. I really just came to say hello. So let's leave it at that."

After a few minutes of casual talk, Nick and I got up to leave. But before we reached the door, the chauffeur quietly pulled me aside. He had overheard the entire conversation and how uncomfortable it made me, and he offered me forty dollars. I declined; it was against my grandmother's wishes, and I did not want him to get in trouble for trying to do me a favor. Instead, I said, "What you can do is give me a piece of cardboard and a marker." A few minutes later, he returned with the items I asked for. "Thanks, JT. You're the best."

After the door closed behind us, Nick asked, "What in the world did you say to him, and why in the world do you have a piece of cardboard and a marker?"

"As soon as we get downstairs, we're going to start heading home," I said. "We're going to make a sign for Fort Lauderdale, Florida. We're hitchhiking. It's our best plan."

It took sixteen rides to leave Chicago. Standing in South Chicago with a cardboard sign reading 'Fort Lauderdale, Florida,' we were looked at like we were crazy. However, we persisted.

We took a total of seventy rides. Using only maps (no GPS at the time), we figured out how to travel through Ohio, Kentucky, and Tennessee. We avoided interstates and relied on back roads, unsure whether hitchhiking was legal in some states.

Most of the people who picked us up were not wealthy. They

were traveling salesmen, people who lived on the road, humble folks, probably two steps away from where we were. But when they heard our story, they helped us. Some bought us lunch. Some let us sleep in their cars. A few handed us ten dollars to keep us going. They were people trying to make it on their own, yet they still reached out to help someone else along.

The last ride ended somewhere in Georgia. We asked where the driver was headed, and he said Fort Lauderdale. I should have been relieved. Instead, I felt a strange sadness that the journey was over. I had been so consumed by the adventure, piecing together each leg and learning the states as we passed through them, funny enough, I was not ready for it to end.

After three days and seventy rides, we finally made it home.

Nick and I were back in Fort Lauderdale, safe and sound, but our summer plans had been spoiled. Still, it was another enriching and exciting adventure.

Now I was ready for one more: my first year at junior college.

College had not always been part of my plan. Unlike Phil, whose mother drilled into him that higher education was non-negotiable, I had no such expectations at home. I had slept through most of high school, exhausted from late nights spent parking cars. My path forward was unclear.

But Phil would not let it rest. "No, no, you have to go to college," he told me. "There is no way around it."

I took Phil's advice to heart. When the time came, I took the state exam required for admission to Florida State. Phil made the score. I did not. While Phil headed to Tallahassee, I enrolled at Broward Junior Community College for a year to improve my grades and try again.

I needed to transform myself from a D student who knew nothing about studying and certainly nothing about algebra or chemistry into someone who was college ready. All I had to do to get into Florida State was raise my grade point average to 2.0 (a C average) and slightly improve my SAT score. I spent nine months, two semesters, at Broward working toward this.

I needed help, and the professors and counselors at Broward quickly became the cure for my academic struggles. Patient and encouraging, they showed me how to study, take notes, and make the most of my time, turning learning into something fun rather than frustrating.

One class stands out. I signed up for speech, thinking it would be easy. It turned out to be one of the most challenging courses I took because I had to stand up and speak in front of people for the first time. I was not used to it.

For my first speech, I chose to speak about polo. I brought in a polo mallet, climbed onto a chair, and demonstrated the different swings: the forehand, the backhand, and the complexities of riding a horse while striking a ball. The students had never seen anything like it. None of them had ever watched a polo match. I invited them to attend a game, and the professor gave me an A+.

That instructor was inspiring. After class, he told me I had potential and should go on to university. It was the first time a teacher had ever said anything like that to me.

Within a few weeks at community college, I found joy in studying. Late at night, under the soft glow of my desk lamp, I eagerly consumed textbooks and assignments one after another; information felt like my lifeblood, the sun in my personal universe. By reducing my parking duties and stopping newspaper delivery, I no longer felt tired during the day, which gave me the energy and motivation to learn.

I became a completely different student, one who was curious and motivated. Instead of going on physical journeys, I found new adventures within the pages of my books, escaping into new worlds of literature, the arts, math, and science. I never realized how much I did not know, but now I do. I enjoyed attending class and discussing the readings with my professors and fellow students.

Junior colleges are ideal for students like me: I was smart, but did not realize what it took to earn good grades. The professors at Broward taught me how to do that, and after one year, I had raised my GPA and SAT score enough to be accepted into Florida State. Once I received my acceptance letter, I called Phil, who was already on campus in Tallahassee. "I'm coming to be your roommate," I told him. Together we cheered in excitement. The two of us were about to be back together again.

All those nights parking cars at The MaiKai and all the miles I traveled on the paper route finally paid off: I had enough money to pay my own way to Florida State, which cost about six hundred dollars per semester. My grandfather had paid for my older siblings' first two years of college, but now that he had passed away, that privilege was not available to me. After my experience with my grandmother in Chicago, I was not expecting any handouts from her. Still, this was how I preferred it, paying my own way. It bolstered the sense of freedom and independence I felt when I first set foot on campus in the fall of 1969.

Why did Phil and I decide to go to Florida State? I will let Phil explain. "My brother was already heading to Florida State when Tim and I visited the school as high school seniors," Phil said. "Florida State was once the state's women's college. The ratio of girls to guys was three to one. I mean, there were pretty girls everywhere when we visited. We thought it was fantastic. We looked at each other and said, 'This is where we're going!' We did not choose it for academics. The school attracted us with all those beautiful, long-legged female students we saw." Yes, it is true: like most young men our age, we were girlcrazy, and Florida State was full of eye-catching beauties.

Phil has a collection of stories from our time together at Florida State. "Tim and I were roommates, and we rented an apartment at the College Cabana Apartments that had just been built," Phil recalled. "My older brother was still on the swim team, and he lived below us. Neither Tim nor I had much money for food, and it was hard for us to pay the electricity bill. But eventually, my brother and I bought an MGM for two hundred dollars, and that became our transportation. Although it was registered in my brother's name, Tim would often drive it.

"You know, Tim ignores stop signs or parking zones. As a result, he received parking tickets all over the campus. One night, the police came and arrested my brother, taking him to jail for all his outstanding parking tickets. The thing was, my brother didn't drive the car, but it was registered in his name because Tim and I weren't allowed to have a vehicle on campus. However, my brother was allowed. So, the police took my brother away. Tim and I had to bail him out of jail, and it was all Tim's fault.

"Tim was a wild driver. He'd drive on sidewalks, park wherever he pleased, even in the teachers' lot. To this day, Tim pays no attention to rules. He doesn't. That's probably part of the reason for his success. There's a direct relationship there."

So one day during my first semester at Florida State, I was walking to class in the Williams Building, which housed the Humanities Department. As I passed the door to the main office, I noticed a few female students standing outside and looking at a small sign on the door that read:

Please Enroll in the Florence Program

I asked one of the co-eds what this program was about. "It's a study abroad program in Florence, Italy," she explained. "Florida State has an extension program there. There's one spot remaining. You should come with us." I was intrigued, partly because of that beautiful young woman, but also because I was seeking another adventure, another opportunity to reinvent myself.

"Sure, I'll go," I told her, even though I knew nothing about Italy. "Do you know how much it costs? Is it affordable?"

She explained that the entire program, including tuition, airfare, books, and accommodations, cost only $1,400. After doing some research, I discovered she was right: everything in Italy was dirt-cheap because the dollar was so strong against the lira.

In Florence, I could get a five-course dinner for about two American dollars. Studying in Italy was actually cheaper than staying in Tallahassee, and the average class size there was just ten students. By contrast, at Florida State, I usually sat in a large auditorium with 150.

She asked me another question: "Have you ever been out of the country before?"

"No," I replied. "I've been to El Paso, Chicago, New Orleans, and New York, but I've never left the United States."

"You need to get a passport," she said, then explained the process.

I had never owned a passport. I had never needed one. But that afternoon, I enrolled in the Florence program and began the application.

While I waited for the passport, I went to the library and pulled every book I could find on Florence. The Uffizi. Michelangelo. The Renaissance. I knew nothing about any of it. As I turned the pages, I knew I had to see it all for myself.

I hurried back to our apartment and told Phil about my impulsive decision. "I'm off to Italy!" I announced. I explained that there were no spots left in the extension program for the spring semester and that I would be leaving in just a few days. But I also stressed that he should come to Florence with me over the summer. We could study in Italy for one, two, or even three more semesters, for as long as we wanted. Nearly as impulsive as I was, Phil eagerly agreed.

As I packed my bags in our apartment, filling my suitcase with shirts, shorts, and pants, I had no idea how much this journey would change me.

On the day I left, I told Phil I would see him in a few months. Then I boarded a plane for the first time in my life. As we took off and soared into the blue sky over the vast waters of the Atlantic Ocean, my spirits lifted even higher.

Just two years earlier, I was a shy, introverted kid with no real dreams beyond maybe managing a valet stand one day. Now I was crossing the Atlantic, heading to a city I had only read about in books.

Eight

Welcome to the Renaissance

Seven days later, that is, after I noticed the group of female students reading a sign outside the Humanities office at Florida State, I was stepping off a plane in Florence, Italy.

My senses were immediately overwhelmed. It was my first time in a foreign country. I did not speak a word of Italian, so I could not understand what the locals were saying unless they spoke English, and I could not read most street signs. Unlike my other adventures, I knew no one in Italy except the students who had told me about the program a week earlier.

I moved into a room at Villa Fabbricotti and immediately found myself among students and professors devoted to the liberal arts. During those first days in Florence, whenever I was not in class, I spent hours wandering the city alone, exploring its trattorias and history.

Florence is often regarded as the birthplace of the Renaissance, the period spanning roughly from 1450 to 1527. Before that, medieval art was largely abstract and formulaic, concerned primarily with telling biblical stories in simple visual terms.

Renaissance art, by contrast, became rational and humanistic. It embraced linear perspective and shading and was created by giants such as Leonardo da Vinci, Donatello, Michelangelo, and Raphael. During this period, art shifted from idealism to realism, and artists began to see themselves as human beings in all their complexity, a view reflected in their work.

I loved touring the museums alone, spending hours immersed in art as I wandered through the Uffizi Gallery, the Palatina Gallery, the Bargello, the Museum of San Marco, and many others. At night, I would slip into an outoftheway pizzeria, savor a few slices of pizza, and linger over a glass or two of red wine.

*Villa Fabbricotti,
Florence. Home to the
Florida State study
abroad program.*

It was in the classroom that I met the man who would become my greatest inspiration in Florence: Professor Fred Licht. He was special. I was convinced he knew more about art and life in Florence than anyone else, and he shared his vast knowledge of Catholic religious art and the Renaissance in the most straightforward, most articulate way imaginable.

He spoke nine languages fluently. Watching him jump from German to Hebrew to French and back to English, sometimes within the same lecture, was extraordinary.

I often spoke with Fred after class and in his office, and he quickly became a mentor. He motivated me more than any other professor I had ever had, pushing me to study in a way I never had before. I overprepared before I walked into his classroom, for fear of disappointing him, ever.

When I learned that Fred was Jewish, I wondered how a Jewish

Professor Fred Litt at the Greek temples, Agrigento, Sicily.

professor could be so deeply knowledgeable about Catholic religious art and so enamored and respectful of it. I soon realized that experiencing and understanding excellence is at the heart of higher education.

Despite being an American, Fred was among the most influential men in Florence. In the fall of 1966, a devastating flood tore through the city. Floods were so rare that more than ninety percent of the population had no warning of the imminent disaster that fateful day. One hundred one people were killed, and entire museums were washed away, making it Florence's worst flood since 1557. Between three and four million books and manuscripts were damaged, along with fourteen thousand pieces of movable art.

It is by no coincidence that this flood caused one of the most interesting times in history, and that I arrived two years after the catastrophic tragedy.

At the time, Fred was teaching in Florence, and he immediately set to work raising money to restore countless artworks and books.

He had developed a close relationship with Peggy Guggenheim, whose uncle, Solomon, has a famous museum named after him in New York City: The Guggenheim. Peggy herself owned the Peggy Guggenheim Collection in Venice, one of the most important museums in the Western world, featuring Cubism, Surrealism, and Abstract Expressionism.

A giant in the art world, Peggy sponsored and collected works by some of the twentieth century's greatest artists, including Picasso, Max Ernst, Joan Miró, and Jackson Pollock.

After the flood, Fred called Peggy for help. She donated millions of dollars, which he administered for restorations, and together they secured millions more from other wealthy Americans through some gentle persuasion.

Thanks to Fred's diligence and persistence, many priceless treasures were saved, and he became something of a folk hero in the Italian art world. One of the best-known stories from that catastrophe involves Donatello's Penitent Magdalene, a magnificent wooden sculpture of Mary Magdalene. As the floodwaters rose, Florentines rushed to museums and churches to rescue priceless works of art. A few locals managed to save the five-hundred-year-old Penitent Magdalene and, after the waters receded, returned it to the Museo dell'Opera del Duomo, tied to the top of a Fiat 500.

Fred loved sharing stories from the flood. They revealed the deep love and pride Italians have for their art and heritage. Through them, the world of art came alive for me and deepened my understanding of art's importance in recording the human condition throughout history.

Fred fundamentally changed me. I had already learned how to study in junior college and understood what it took to succeed, but in Florence, everything shifted. Because of him, I became a straight-A student. Fred inspired me to study, and I began to crave information with a hunger I had never felt before. His passion influenced me profoundly, and as one of his best students, I was rewarded in turn.

One day, we drove from Florence to Venice and had lunch with Peggy Guggenheim at Palazzo Venier dei Leoni on the Grand Canal, home to her renowned collection. As we dined, I sat in awe across from such a prominent figure in the art world. Just two years earlier, I had been parking cars and sleeping through classes in Fort Lauderdale; I never could have imagined this moment.

After our afternoon with Peggy, we headed back to Florence. As he always did, Fred shared his world with me. From behind the wheel, he pointed out details along the road and wove in stories, always teaching and sharing his knowledge.

His deep involvement in restoring some of Florence's most remarkable works of art also meant that he was on a first-name basis with Luciano Bausi, the mayor of Florence. In the months that followed, Fred pulled some strings and received special permission from the mayor for me to lead tour groups through museums like the Uffizi Gallery. Normally, this required licenses, permits, and specialized training. It was an unprecedented opportunity, and Fred opened that door because he trusted me. He was, in short, my Italian version of Bud Heatley.

Six months after I arrived in Italy, Phil joined me and moved into my villa. Almost at once, he noticed how much I had changed.

"We used to call Tim 'the professor' because, suddenly, he was an amazing student in Italy," Phil recalled. "Tim had never excelled in school before, except for a brief stint in junior college. He's brilliant, but he used to sleep through high school because he worked nights parking cars.

"When he met his professor, Fred Licht, something clicked. Tim became fully immersed in his studies and in the city of Florence, even growing a beard to look the part. He was completely different from the Tim I knew before.

"For the rest of college, he stayed focused and did extremely well. I believe it all goes back to that special professor in Florence. It's amazing how one person can have such a profound impact on another's life."

Phil was right. I became an entirely new person in Florence.

Florence, 1969.

After some time had passed and Phil had caught up on his studies after arriving in Florence, the two of us gave tours of the Uffizi, the Pitti Palace, the Bargello, Santa Croce, and the Giotto Chapel.

Leading those tours not only deepened my appreciation for art; it also began to change the way I saw myself.

Imagine this: a nineteen year old from Florida lecturing fifty students in the Uffizi about the subtle differences between Giotto's Madonna and Child and Cimabue's Madonna Enthroned, or standing before the group, explaining the intellectual and economic forces that sparked the Renaissance.

The students were enthralled, almost as if I were a priest and they were my congregation. People rarely recognize their own transformation as it happens; it usually becomes clear only in hindsight. But in that moment, I realized something profound was happening. My personal growth, stunted for years in my small Fort Lauderdale world, was now accelerating in Florence, and I loved every moment of it. I am no longer sitting on that bench.

"Once Tim found his way to Florence, he finally found himself," said my sister, Judy.

Like any adventurer, I did not limit where I would explore.

When spring break arrived, a group of us left Italy and took a train to London, where we stayed at a bed-and-breakfast in Golders Green run by a wonderful woman named Mrs. Pister, who treated us like family. At the time, it cost $1.50 a night. People slept on the staircases in sleeping bags. Travelers coming and going would leave their gear for the next person. It was a community, a waystation for wanderers.

On the first night, the students I was with gathered in a room to plan our itinerary for the next few days. Everyone wanted to tour the city and visit major attractions such as Madame Tussaud's, everyone except me. I never saw myself as a tourist. I was an adventurer, and I planned to explore off the beaten path, whether anyone came with me or not.

As I told the group I would not be joining their citywide tour, I noticed a young woman nodding along. It was my classmate, Sue Brett, a striking blonde. She had caught the same wanderlust I felt, and after a brief conversation, the two of us agreed to explore Europe and beyond together, just us, no tour group, no agenda.

This was spontaneous. I had already made an impulsive decision when I enrolled in the study abroad program and traveled to a place I had never been to study a subject I had barely considered. Now I was making another quick choice, mainly because the first one had turned out so well. I was only twenty, but I was starting to trust my instincts and let them guide me, even though most of my classmates were more cautious and reserved. I had found a beautiful partner to be my fellow adventurer.

About ten hours after we first talked about exploring together, Sue and I were on our way.

We bought a BSA Starfire, a four-stroke motorcycle that became our chariot across Europe, through the Strait of Gibraltar, and into Africa. To pay for the Starfire, Sue cashed in her Eurail Pass, and I contributed the rest of the money I had saved from delivering newspapers and parking cars in Fort Lauderdale. We chose a motorcycle because we did not want the restrictions of the Eurail. We wanted to go wherever we chose, whenever we chose.

Sue was petite, and Starfire was nearly three times her size, yet she quickly mastered it, flying down the road like Evel Knievel, weaving in and out of lanes and around sharp curves with effortless grace. I was usually at the handlebars, but my favorite moments were when I sat behind her, my arms wrapped around her as her blonde hair streamed in the wind and the world blurred past us, two travelers on a roaring machine in a foreign land.

We sped through the English countryside, took a ferry to France, and drove into Paris. With Sue on the back, we arrived at the Arc de Triomphe, one of the most famous monuments in the City of Light, standing at the western end of the ChampsÉlysées in the center of Place Charles de Gaulle. The Arc sits at the intersection of twelve radiating avenues, and it was challenging to navigate around the Citroëns and Peugeots circling the monument, especially when we could not stop staring at it.

Commissioned in 1806 after the victory at Austerlitz, the Arc was ordered by Emperor Napoleon Bonaparte at the height of his power. Over the years, it has witnessed many famous victory marches: the Germans in 1871, the French in 1919, the Germans in 1940, and the French and their Allies in 1944 and 1945. History felt very real as we walked through the monument and looked down at the Tomb of the Unknown Soldier from World War I, which lies directly beneath it. Placed there on Armistice Day in 1920, it holds the first eternal flame lit in Western or Eastern Europe since the Vestal Virgins' fire was extinguished in the fourth century. The flame burns in memory of those who died but were never identified in either World War. Sue and I were deeply moved.

Our exploration was only beginning. After a few unforgettable days in Paris, strolling along the Seine and marveling at landmarks like the Eiffel Tower, we climbed back aboard the Starfire. We followed the Mediterranean coast toward Spain. I had never seen water so beautiful; it shimmered with the color of the deepest, clearest sky.

We stopped in Perpignan, founded in the early tenth century, and wandered through the Cathedral of Saint John the Baptist. It took nearly 175 years to complete, finally being finished in 1509. I could not get enough of Europe's culture and history; America felt so new compared with what we encountered each day on our journey.

Leaving Perpignan, I spotted a sign for Barcelona: forty-five miles. It was five o'clock, and I was sure we could make it by sunset. I had forgotten one crucial detail: the Pyrenees, the massive mountain range that forms the border between France and Spain. Instead of a quick dash south, we spent hours on twisting, turning roads, climbing and descending the mountains.

The temperature dropped as we climbed. By nightfall, we were too high in the mountains to stop and sleep. We had to push through to a warmer climate. The wind cut through us at seventy miles an hour. When we finally stopped for coffee somewhere near midnight, I realized my beard and mustache had frozen into a single block of ice. I could barely get the cup to my lips.

The detour cost us daylight, but we finally arrived in Barcelona seven hours later, at 2 a.m.

I learned a valuable lesson. Even when you act on impulse, you still need to be prepared. I had not studied a map and did not realize we had a daunting mountain range ahead. This time, my lack of preparation did not put us in harm's way. We would not be so lucky a few days later.

We continued along the coast of Spain, taking our time and savoring the scenery. We had almost no money, so we lived off the land. I remember picking oranges straight from the fields and eating them for lunch. During the day, we explored seaside towns; at night, we slept on beaches under the stars. We never spent a single night in a hotel the entire trip.

Sue and I were having the best time of our lives. I especially loved those moments before sleep, staring up at the sky and thinking about how far I had come from that shy boy who had left for junior college just eighteen months earlier.

Now I was living a life I had never imagined in Fort Lauderdale. I had barely known this part of the world existed, and here I was, eager to see more, experience more, live more. I felt full of confidence, joy, and curiosity. I had never believed I could be this happy. Even my wildest dreams had not come close.

We reached the Rock of Gibraltar, a massive limestone promontory in the British Territory of Gibraltar, near the southwestern tip of Europe. According to ancient myth, the Rock, which rises 1,398 feet, was one of two points marking the edge of the known world.

We loved exploring the maze of tunnels the British had carved inside. Although the Rock covers only 2.6 square miles, Gibraltar holds about thirty-four miles of tunnels. The British used this underground fortress to house up to sixteen thousand men, along with the supplies, ammunition, and equipment needed to withstand a long siege. During World War II, the Rock was a key stronghold for defending shipping routes into the Mediterranean.

We devoured every scrap of information we could find about the Rock. But I had a more urgent concern: we were nearly out of money.

In Spain, we found a Western Union office, and I telegraphed my mother in Fort Lauderdale, asking her to send seventy-five dollars. When the money arrived, it was only fifteen dollars. The mistake was mine. In Europe, sevens are written with a slash. I wrote my seven without the slash, and the Western Union clerk misread it as a one, turning 75 into 15. The missing sixty dollars stung, but the road was calling louder than our money worries.

We climbed back on the motorcycle and took off again, short on money but high on the thrill of the road. We crossed into Morocco, which felt like traveling back in time. We toured Casablanca, Fez, and Meknes, the ancient capital, staying as far off the tourist trail as possible. This was exactly what we wanted: to visit places most Americans would not even dare to try.

We were naïve. I was a bearded college kid in jeans, and Sue was a dimpled blonde in cutoff shorts and a tank top. We looked like American hippies, free-spirited nonconformists in a traditional Arabic setting. We did not realize the trouble our appearance might bring.

Late one night, we were in a café when a Moroccan general approached us. We invited him to join our table, and after an extended chat, he asked us back to his barracks. We had no lodging planned, and a free night was too good to pass up. We accepted.

We followed the general on our motorcycle to the barracks. It did not take long for me to realize how dangerous the situation had become. The general's demeanor shifted, and it quickly became clear he intended to spend some one-on-one time with Sue, with or without her consent. I let her know we had to get out of there, and now.

As soon as the general and his soldiers were out of sight, we bolted, running toward the Starfire. We pushed the motorcycle quietly down a rocky road and into the cover of the nearby woods. Once we were hidden, we jumped on, and I started the engine, which was loud enough to stir up the general and his soldiers.

We sped away, glancing over our shoulders to see troops in Jeeps racing after us. Our hearts pounded, adrenaline surged, and we knew we would be caught if we stayed on the main roads. I jerked the wheel and veered off the beaten path, driving deeper into the woods and onto ground the Jeeps could not navigate.

In hindsight, it feels exhilarating, the story of our Great Escape. In the moment, though, we were terrified, bouncing over rocks and roots in the dark, desperate to outrun the general and his soldiers. We had no idea where we would end up, but that was part of the thrill we both enjoyed.

Only miles later did I begin to see our role in what nearly became a disaster. Savvy visitors to Morocco understand that it is proper to wear traditional dress: a djellaba, the loose, robe-like garment worn over clothes. We were ignorant of this and failed to honor local customs. We nearly paid a steep price for that oversight.

When Sue and I began our journey on the rain-slicked streets of overcast London, our dream was to reach the Great Pyramids of Egypt. We never made it that far. Eventually, the semester called us back, and we had to return to Florence for class. Even so, we traveled more than four thousand miles on our trusty Starfire, south from London to Morocco and then back to Florence. Over those two weeks, I had never felt so alive, so free, so utterly at peace with my place in the world.

Our situation became clear when we arrived in Pisa to refuel the motorcycle. I reached into my pocket and realized I only had a single Kennedy half dollar left.

I showed the coin to the attendant. His eyes brightened. In the late 1960s, John F. Kennedy was greatly admired by Italians as the first Catholic President of the United States. I handed him the half dollar, and he gently traced its surface as if feeling Kennedy's face. He filled our tank completely and told us not to worry about the rest of the payment. He was happy to accept the fifty-cent piece. I shook his hand, and we set off excitedly toward Florence.

Like every great adventure, my trip with Sue taught me a lot. We improvised every day, making things up as we went along. We learned to live off the land, often catching our own fish, to be resourceful, and the importance of focusing on solutions rather than dwelling on problems. Most importantly, I discovered a fundamental truth: true happiness does not require money. When you are willing to put yourself out there and take chances, the randomness of life can be incredibly exciting on its own.

Once we returned, I dropped Sue off at her apartment. We hugged, long and tight, and I felt it was both an ending and a beginning. It marked the close of our journey over land and sea and signaled the start of my new life: one defined by risk-taking, experimentation, and an unrelenting search for new adventures.

Crossing the Alps by motorcycle, May 1972.

I was not finished with the Starfire, not by a long shot. Travel and adventure had taken hold of me, and I needed more.

When I had a few days off from classes and my tour-guide responsibilities, I asked Phil to come along to Greece. It took him a second to reply: "Hell yes."

We took the ferry from Florence to Piraeus and then guided the Starfire toward Athens. Arriving in the city, often called the birthplace of Western civilization and democracy, was breathtaking.

Athens is one of the world's oldest cities, with a recorded history stretching back more than 3,400 years and evidence of human presence dating back from the 11th to the 7th millennia BC.

On our first night, we camped on the Hill of the Muses, directly across from the marvelous citadel. From our campsite, we had a spectacular view of the Acropolis, the rocky outcrop above the city, crowned with ancient buildings, including the Parthenon.

At night, the Parthenon glowed against the dark sky, visible for miles. Built in the fifth century BCE, this former temple is adorned with sculptures that are among the high points of Greek art and enduring symbols of democracy. As I gazed at the Parthenon, I imagined those distant days when the seeds of the government we embrace today in America were first planted. In that quiet moment, history felt alive to me.

The next day, we explored the city before boarding another ferry to Heraklion, Crete's main port. We were giddy with anticipation. In the 1960s, this ancient island was the ultimate hippie haven, with its clear waters and sandy beaches drawing free spirits from around the world.

As soon as we arrived, we headed straight for the manmade caves above the fishing village of Matala. Carved out of soft stone thousands of years ago, these tiny caves became an iconic symbol of my generation, simple, sheltered hollows that were perfect for unrolling a sleeping bag.

For the hippies, the highlight of each day was watching the sunset, a ritual they treated with almost religious reverence. We arrived just in time for the most mystical sunset of all: the spring equinox. As the sun sank, the sky erupted in a stunning, spellbinding blaze of color so vivid that several people were moved to tears. Even now, that fiery, beautiful sky remains etched in my memory forever.

By day, the crowded beach and small town were alive with people like me, adventurers eager to savor this one-of-a-kind place. At night, the caves glowed with dancing firelight. We lit bonfires and watched the waves roll in below. Some people sang, others played guitars or Greek bouzoukis. Among the travelers was Joni Mitchell, who spent several months in Matala in 1969. Two songs from her album Blue, "Carey" and "California," were inspired by her time there.

Trips like this one with Phil and my four-thousand-mile journey with Sue reshaped how I saw the world. Life is meant to be lived, not just observed. It should be experienced, felt, and explored. Beauty is everywhere if we are brave enough to look for it.

The tours I led at the Uffizi also left a deep mark on me. Botticelli, Cimabue, Leonardo, and Michelangelo became vivid presences in my life because I spent so many hours talking about them and their works. To understand their motivations, goals, and gifts, I had to step into their minds. Over time, they began to feel like friends.

Then came an unexpected call. My mother phoned from Fort Lauderdale to say she wanted to visit me in Italy. I had never tried to impress an adult family member in my life, but I was thrilled that she wanted to see me and perhaps recognize how much I had changed since boarding that plane in Tallahassee nearly two years earlier.

It was my mother's first trip to Europe. The night she arrived in Florence coincided with a jazz concert for one of our tour groups in the Salone dei Cinquecento, the Hall of Five Hundred, at the Palazzo Vecchio. I asked if she wanted to come along. "Of course," she replied.

Mayor Bausi hosted the evening. After the performance, he stepped into the spotlight to give a speech, and halfway through, he unexpectedly called my name, inviting me to come forward. Surprised, I approached him to a round of applause, completely unsure of what was going on.

Then, in front of the crowd and my mother, he presented me with a jeweled fleur-de-lis, the symbol of Florence, set with a ruby in gold. Blushing and still bewildered, I accepted the gift and thanked him.

The mayor told the audience that he was giving me the fleur-de-lis to honor my service as an Ambassador of Florence to Americans and to American tourism. The crowd erupted in applause again.

I stepped off the stage and went straight to my mother. She had sacrificed so much to give my siblings and me the best life she could. Life had not been easy for her, but she always did her best.

Tears streamed down her face as I approached. I was still holding the pin from the mayor when I placed it in her hand. She looked at it, then at me, and pulled me into a hug tighter than any she had ever given me.

She wore that pin proudly for the rest of her life. When she passed, it was still there, fastened over her heart, as if she had never let go of that special moment.

With Mom at Piazza San Marco, Venice.

Nine

My First Taste of the Culinary World

I never went back to graduate from Florida State University's Tallahassee campus. Instead, after arriving in Florence, I decided to stay there for two years, immersing myself in new cultures, people, perspectives, and adventures.

My 1970 graduation ceremony was held in the Tuscan hills near Florence, where a small group of about twelve students gathered. I wore a Moroccan coat with fur trim, similar to what hippies liked. I earned a B.A. in art history from Florida State, and afterward, Phil and I remained in Florence for a few more months, leading tours across Tuscany.

One day, after finishing a tour for a group of Americans, I returned home to find a letter in my mailbox. It was from Uncle Sam: the draft board was ordering me to report for duty at the U.S. Army base in Pisa, Italy, to prepare for the Vietnam War. I had been drafted.

I walked the streets of Florence that night, thinking about what I had been asked to do. I was studying Michelangelo, the David, and the beauty he had created over five hundred years ago. And now I was being asked to pick up a rifle and fight in the rice paddies of a country I knew nothing about, for a cause I did not believe in. The juxtaposition was too stark to ignore.

Even my brother, a United States Marine who had served two tours in Vietnam and earned a Purple Heart, told me the truth. "This war is a mess," he said. "Do everything you can to avoid involvement."

I did my research. I learned that Muhammad Ali had fought his case all the way to the Supreme Court and won. He was a prizefighter, a man who made his living in a violent sport, yet he was granted conscientious objector status because he held the belief in nonviolence as strongly as any religious conviction. The Supreme Court broadened the definition. It was not tied to any specific religion. If you held the belief deeply and sincerely, you could qualify.

A quote from John F. Kennedy stayed with me: "Until the prestige of the conscientious objector parallels that of the war hero, there will be no end to war." That was powerful. A president had said those words.

My statement quoted Kennedy and described Michelangelo's beauty. I argued that mankind's power to create beauty would far outlast any war. David is five hundred years old and still draws millions. Art can teach us so much more than war.

The risk was real. If the draft board denied my application and I still refused to serve, I could face up to five years in prison. Muhammad Ali had been convicted and stripped of his title before his appeal succeeded. But I had made up my mind.

When I appeared before the local draft board, I brought my dolly, Kathy, with me. She was a Catholic nun. I do not know whether that impressed them or my statement did, but they granted me conscientious objector status on the first try. I had prepared to fight all the way to the top, but I did not have to.

My assignment was an alternative service at the International Quaker Center in Paris. The Quakers were doing remarkable work. While the governments of North and South Vietnam met in Paris to negotiate peace, the Quaker Center held parallel meetings with people on both sides.

There, I worked as a cook, preparing simple meals for the attendees. Rice, potatoes, and the occasional sausage baked into a casserole. It was my first real introduction to French cuisine, and I began learning the language that would later prove essential to my career.

I could have been in Vietnam. Instead, I was in Paris, cooking for people who were trying to bring peace. It was a humbling and rewarding time.

While volunteering at the Quaker Center, I spotted an advertisement in the Herald Tribune for English-speaking actors in a play. I had a few hours free in the afternoon, so I walked over to audition. I thought it might be a way to meet some new people and have a little fun.

The play, titled "The Serpent, The Ceremony" by Jean-Claude Van Itallie, was sponsored by the American Embassy. A young director from Berkeley had come to Paris to stage it. The story explored Eve's temptation in the Garden of Eden, then leaped forward to the 1960s, weaving in the assassinations of John F. Kennedy and Martin Luther King. It was part theater, part dance, part street performance.

We opened each show in the streets of Paris itself. Our lead actor would emerge, blowing fire from his mouth, while a clarinet player filled the air with sensuous jazz. Curious Parisians would gather, and we would slowly lead them through the winding streets near Saint-Germain-des-Prés, down into our small basement theater. It felt revolutionary, as if we were part of something important.

At the audition, I met a young man studying at the École Internationale de Théâtre Jacques Lecoq, one of Paris's great mime schools. Like so many in his craft, he was inspired by the legendary Marcel Marceau. His name was Avner Eisenberg, a big Jewish kid from Atlanta, Georgia. He stood six feet four with a thick beard, and he was absolutely brilliant. I had never seen anyone move the way he did. Every gesture was precise, every expression perfectly controlled. This guy was a quintessential mime artist, the real thing.

We became friends over the following weeks, rehearsing together, grabbing cheap meals when we could, and wandering the city when we could not.

One Sunday morning, Avner and I met near the Seine. Neither of us had any money. I mean, flat broke. Not a franc between us. The kind of broke where you count the hours until your next meal and hope something turns up.

But Avner had an idea.

"Let us put on a show," he said. "Near the Eiffel Tower. Sunday morning, lots of tourists."

It sounded reasonable. He had the skills. I would help however I could.

We walked to the Champ de Mars, that long green lawn stretching from the Ecole Militaire to the Eiffel Tower. The morning light was soft and golden, as Paris looks in old photographs. Families strolled with children. Couples sat on benches. Tourists craned their necks upward at the iron lattice towering above.

Avner found a spot with good foot traffic.

He began with subtle movements that caught the eye of a few passersby. A woman stopped. Then a man. Then a small cluster of people. Avner had this gift. He could draw a crowd without saying a word, without making a sound. His body told stories. He became trapped in an invisible box. He walked against an invisible wind. He pulled an invisible rope.

The crowd kept growing. In Paris, when a small gathering forms, curiosity spreads like wildfire. People see a crowd and want to know what everyone is looking at. Soon we had two hundred people, maybe three hundred, all pressed together, watching this big-bearded American perform silent magic beneath the Eiffel Tower.

I stood at the edge, watching Avner work, feeling hopeful for the first time in weeks. Maybe we will eat well tonight. Maybe things were turning around.

Then I heard it.

That sound. The unique European police siren. Not the American wail, but that distinctive two-tone pulse. Ba-da, ba-da, ba-da. Far away at first, then growing closer.

I felt it in my gut before I understood it in my head. That siren was for us.

Paris in the early 1970s was still raw from the 1968 riots. The police did not like large crowds gathering unexpectedly. They did not know whether it was a protest, a demonstration, or a political action. Three hundred people gathered that Sunday morning, raised alarms.

The siren grew louder. Ba-da, ba-da, ba-da.

I looked at Avner. He was deep in his performance, eyes half-closed, hands sculpting invisible shapes in the air. The crowd was transfixed. He had no idea.

I did something unforgivable. Something that violates the most sacred rule of mime. I broke the silence.

"Avner," I said. "The siren is for us."

He stopped. The invisible box vanished. The invisible wind died. He turned and looked at me, and his expression said it all. It was like Moses throwing down the tablets among the sinners. How dare you? How dare you break the silence? That is the one thing you never do. He did not say a word. He did not have to.

But I was right.

Five minutes later, a police van pulled up. Officers pushed through the crowd, which scattered like pigeons. They grabbed Avner and me and shoved us into the back of the van. The doors slammed shut.

Through the small window, I watched the Eiffel Tower shrink as we drove away.

At the station, the police were not quite sure what to make of us. Two young Americans. No weapons. No political pamphlets. No drugs. We had not robbed anyone or hurt anyone. We had simply gathered a crowd.

They searched through old law books for something to charge us with. Finally, they found it. An archaic ordinance from another century.

The charge: can you say it?

Pour faire la bouffonnerie dans la rue

—

"making a buffoon of yourself in public."

I still have a copy of that arrest warrant somewhere.

While the officer typed up the paperwork, hunting and pecking at the keys, Avner could not help himself. He began miming the typewriter. His fingers moved in perfect synchronization with the officer's, his face mirroring the concentration, the frustration, and the occasional pause to think. Some of the other officers started laughing. A few just shook their heads. These crazy Americans.

They held us for a couple of hours, then let us go with a warning. I promised not to make a buffoon of myself in the street again.

But sitting in that police station, watching Avner mime the typewriter, something shifted inside me. I looked at my life clearly, maybe for the first time.

I thought about the hunger. The nights when my stomach growled so loudly I could not sleep. The English lessons I gave for five francs, barely enough to buy pommes frites, French fries. The uncertainty of never knowing where my next meal would come from.

And I made a decision.

I was not going to be an artist. I was not going to be a mime. This was not my path. I was going to go into the restaurant business, where I would always be close to kitchens or food and would never again have to wonder whether I would eat tonight.

Avner and I eventually parted ways. He stayed with mime. I returned to America and found my way into kitchens and then restaurants. We lost touch, as young friends often do.

Thirty years later, in 1992, I attended a gala at the Tampa Lowry

Park Zoo. Mime artists performed throughout the evening, weaving among guests in white face paint and black clothing. After one performance, I approached a young woman and told her I had once performed mime in Paris with someone who had a God-given gift and was destined to become a star.

"What was his name?" she asked.

"Avner Eisenberg," I said. "You probably do not know him. It was a long time ago."

Her eyes widened. "The Avner Eisenberg? He had become one of the world's best mime artists, with a one-man Broadway show, and he also captured all the attention in the movie "Jewel of the Nile," where he was the one carrying the jewel."

I smiled. I was proud to know that my buddy Avner had made it. I thought back to that Sunday morning beneath the Eiffel Tower, two broke kids unsure where life would take us.

He chose silence. I chose flavor.

We both chose right.

After spending a year in Paris, the Army gave me another assignment: relocate to Denver, Colorado, to assist with environmental projects.

One of these projects involved building bicycle lanes, which still exist today. Another was working at one of the country's first recycling centers. In 1971, no one recycled.

We established collection points at grocery stores for glass, newspapers, tin, and aluminum, and I drove the truck that collected them. It was humble work, but important. Today, recycling is common, but we were trailblazers in the beginning.

At the time, I did not own a car and relied on a 20-speed bicycle, riding it everywhere. As I pedaled through the city, I often looked up at the snow-capped Rocky Mountains, towering so high that they seemed to kiss the edge of heaven, and I dreamed of one day living among those peaks.

That day finally came when I received another letter from the Army, telling me my conscientious service was over. With my military service completed, I began looking toward new opportunities.

In the fall of 1972, I bought a cheap car and set out for a new adventure in the Rockies. I drove into Aspen, an old mining town with dirt roads crossing through downtown. Aspen in the early 1970s was very different from what it is now. It was a small town where everyone knew each other by first name.

Phil invited me out. A friend of his who lived there said he could help us find work and get settled. But when we arrived, the friend never showed. Phil decided to head back to El Paso to finish his degree. I stayed.

Aspen was a tough place to find work. Everyone was there for the season, all chasing the same jobs. Housing was just as hard. I ended up living in a little red schoolhouse that served students during the day and became my home at night. You did what you had to do.

I took whatever work I could find. I cleaned chimneys, scraping out soot and ash from fireplace areas in hotel rooms. I cleaned restrooms at the Aspen Mining Company, a popular restaurant and nightclub. I cleaned rooms at the Pomegranate Inn.

Every morning, I watched guests head off to the slopes with skis on their backs while I went the other way, covered in grime. The contrast was hard to ignore. But I was not going anywhere. I was determined to make it work.

A few months after working at the Pomegranate Inn, I got a big break. While at a bar, I overheard a man speaking French and decided to strike up a conversation. I must have impressed him, because he told me he had just become the head chef at the Aspen Institute, a nonprofit dedicated to promoting "a free, just, and equitable society." He offered me a job cooking with him and promised to teach me the fundamentals of French cuisine. I eagerly accepted.

The chef's name was Michel Poumay. He was born in France and raised in Belgium. At age 12, he began working in the hotel kitchen where his father was employed. He later trained at the École d'Hôtellerie de Liège-Culinary in Belgium.

We spent that whole winter together, just the two of us in the kitchen. I was his sous chef. We made eighty meals a night. He taught me the Continental standards: Crêpes Suzette, Steak Diane. But it was his ability to elevate the simplest foods that sparked my imagination. We made croissants from scratch, rolling out the dough by hand. It was difficult, painstaking work, but Michel insisted on doing it right.

One evening, Michel took me to dinner. Because he earned good money, he always paid, while I had almost nothing. He looked at the wine list and chose a bottle. "I will order this one," he said.

I checked the price, and it was $200! I asked, "Why don't you lend me that money instead?" I explained, "I could buy a pair of skis, pay you back, and start skiing tomorrow."

Michel shook his head. "I am going to teach you a lesson," he said. "We are going to buy this wine. You will remember this Château Lafite for the rest of your life. A pair of skis you will soon forget."

He was right. I still remember that wine, that dinner, and the lesson it taught me about quality. Experiences matter more than possessions. That understanding influenced everything I later did with food.

I began to think of endless ways to flavor different foods. As a boy and young man, I viewed food as something to eat. My mother was not much of a cook, and while I enjoyed good meals in Italy and across Europe, I never thought about working in the food industry. But Michel changed everything. Suddenly, he ignited a passion in me I did not even realize I had.

The only other adult male figure who had this kind of impact on my life was Bud Heatley, Phil's father. Now I found myself working side by side with another man whose influence would stay with me throughout my career.

By the end of that winter, I had built a good life. I cooked at night and skied all day. But Aspen is a seasonal place. So when the season ended, Michel and I parted on good terms, as everyone does in a ski town.

Chef Michel eventually opened the renowned Chez Grand-mère in Snowmass, Colorado, which earned the prestigious AAA Four Diamond Award four times. He also cooked for the Chancellor of Germany and the Queen of England. A six-time Mobil 3-Star restaurateur, an honor reserved for some of the world's top chefs, Chef Michel opened my eyes to the endless possibilities of creating flavor.

Many years later, I called him. He had opened a crepe shop in Durango called Michel's Crepe Area and had been running it for years. He was excited to hear about my success, and I was grateful to tell him how much he had shaped it.

After working at the Aspen Institute, I decided to take a road trip to Massachusetts to visit my old friend Phil. He was working at Harvard at the time and had an apartment on Beacon Street in

Boston. He invited me to visit, and I did not hesitate.

I arrived in Boston without a job and with little of a plan. The country was in the grip of the oil embargo, and the economy had ground to a halt. Gas stations were open only two hours a week. You needed a special license plate to fill up on odd or even days, and even then, you were rationed a few gallons. Long lines stretched around the block. No one was hiring.

Midway through an interview with an international wine company, the interviewer began asking me about Florence, including shopping spots and attractions. Finally, I asked her, "What are my chances of getting this job?" She smiled and said, "Oh, we don't have any positions. I am going to Florence and need some suggestions." That was the job market in 1973.

One morning, at Phil's apartment just outside Boston, I was flipping through the Boston Globe when a job ad caught my eye: "Want to drive a new Thunderbird? Have money in your pocket?"

Yes. Yes, I did.

After all, I still aimed to become a polo player someday, and I needed a way to afford this costly pastime, even though I had never played in a polo match. I replied to the ad and headed to a Holiday Inn in Boston for an interview. The ad did not include the company name, and I had no idea that I was applying for a job at Steak & Ale.

The introductory interview went well, and a few days later, I flew to Dallas to interview for a management trainee role at Steak and Ale, a restaurant chain started by Norman Brinker.

When I told Phil I had been hired by Steak & Ale, he smiled. "Norman Brinker," he said. "He is a good friend of my father. We have both sold him horses." That is the polo community. Tight-knit. Connected. Paths always crossing.

Brinker was a giant in the restaurant world. Not only did he found Steak & Ale, but he also served as president of Jack in the Box, helped establish Bennigan's, and would one day be responsible for the growth of more than 1,500 Chili's restaurants worldwide.

Norman revolutionized how people consumed food in the United States and beyond. With Steak & Ale, he introduced the concept of modern casual dining. He pioneered the salad bar, a first-of-its-kind concept in which patrons served themselves, and he was the first to have his waitstaff greet patrons by saying, "Hi, my name is ___ and

I will be your server tonight." These innovations created a more relaxed, laid-back dining experience, and they stuck.

Steak and Ale was recruiting, primarily targeting college-aged men and women for general manager roles, a novel approach at the time. Unlike conventional industry norms, possessing a college degree was required, as Norman sought to portray a youthful, energetic, and tidy image. Previously, casual dining restaurants were mostly family-operated establishments catering to local workers. Norman's tactic changed the industry standard, leading the entire casual dining sector to rapidly adopt this new model.

On my flight to Dallas for an interview, I had no idea Norman shared my passion for polo. A few years later, in 1976, his Willow Bend team won the U.S. Open, the sport's top tournament, and secured the Silver Cup four more times. Norman became a mentor who influenced my life both on the polo field and in the food industry. I would not have met him if I had not impulsively flown across the country to visit Phil. Once again, my adventurous spirit proved valuable.

I performed well in the interview and was offered a management trainee position at Steak & Ale. Did I ever imagine I would work in casual dining? Never. But was I open to it? Absolutely. An essential trait of an adventurer is embracing the journey and letting it unfold naturally. It is like a leaf carried on an autumn breeze, let go and see where the wind takes you. Once you land, the key is to work as hard as you can to make the most of the unexpected opportunity, and that is precisely what I did.

I was assigned to a restaurant just outside Washington, D.C. The training was intense. A hundred hours a week, sometimes more. They started me as a dishwasher for a week, then moved me to the grill, then to the line. The goal was to learn every station and every role from the ground up. When you finally managed your own people, you understood exactly how hard the work was.

I thrived on it. Within six months, I was promoted. Steak & Ale was growing fast, and I knew food. Unlike other college graduates who had never set foot in a kitchen, I could step into any station and hold my own. Michel had prepared me well.

Not long after, some executives invited me on a ski vacation. Norman was there. We skied together as a group during the day, and at night, I found myself sitting at the dining room table with the man who had built this company from the ground up.

I told him about my dream of becoming a polo player. Norman listened, then gave me an honest answer. "Running restaurants is eighty hours a week," he said. "You do not have much time for polo."

He was not trying to discourage me. He was telling me the truth. But I had made up my mind. No matter where my career took me, whether with Norman, Steak & Ale, or anyone else, I was not going to let go of the reins.

But something even more meaningful happened during that time: I met Chris Sullivan, who would become a lifelong friend and later one of the four co-founders of Outback Steakhouse alongside me.

Chris Sullivan was the general manager, and the perfect one at that. He gave clear direction, hired a great staff, and ran one of the best restaurants in the entire chain. He worked me hard, 100 hours a week, but it was all for the best education. Chris would later become the most important partner in my restaurant career.

"Tim and I hit it off the minute we met," Chris recalls. "At that time, I was working in the Washington, D.C. area, managing one of the top Steak n Ale restaurants in the country. It was located in Rockville, Maryland, and was called the Jolly Ox. Maryland and Virginia were two of the few states where the company couldn't use the word 'ale' in the name, so that's why it was named the Jolly Ox."

"Tim was a management trainee, and I was the general manager of that Steak and Ale. He and I just clicked, two Irish guys who loved food and drinks. We became friends right away, and no matter where life took us, we kept that connection. I loved Tim's attitude. I loved his energy. His passion for life was incredible."

Steak & Ale launched my career. Without that training program, practical experience, and mentorship from Chris Sullivan, it is unlikely anyone outside my family and a few close friends would have known my name or my culinary work.

I never advanced very far in the Steak & Ale chain; my highest position was general manager, while Chris rose to vice president. But my interactions with Chris changed the course of my career.

I left Steak & Ale to move to New Orleans and focus on spices and flavors that are my specialty. Yet Chris and I stayed in touch, believing that one day the time might be right to collaborate on something big.

After working for five years in Rockville, Maryland, I moved to Tennessee to oversee a Steak & Ale in the small town of Goodlettsville, just outside Nashville, with a population of 20,000.

Nashville was the heart of country music, and I was a kid from Fort Lauderdale who had wandered the streets of Florence and soaked in the jazz of New Orleans. It was a different world for me.

In Goodlettsville, George Biel managed the Steak & Ale restaurant, focusing intensely on two main priorities: flavor and cleanliness.

One Friday night, as I was closing the place, two guys wearing ski masks entered the restaurant. One of them had a .45-caliber pistol with a silencer and demanded that I hand over all the money in the register. I did exactly as he asked. I was unarmed and the only person there, and then they ran out the door with the cash.

The police came. I answered their questions, filed reports, and did not leave until after 3 a.m. The next day, Saturday, I was back at the restaurant, helping with the investigation while keeping the place running. By Sunday morning, I was exhausted but thankful I had not been hurt. The robbery had left me shaken.

That night, George Biel entered the restaurant and glanced around. Our sales were slow, and one of the five dining rooms was closed off because we did not need the space. George inspected the empty room, found a cigarette butt on the mantel, called me over, and inquired why it had not been appropriately disposed of by the cleaning staff or by me.

By that time, I was drained and still shaken. "We don't use this dining room," I told George. "The cleaning crew probably didn't even enter here; they likely took a shortcut. I'll discuss it with them." He was not convinced. "And what about that cigarette butt?" he asked. "I already explained that," I responded. "But what about the cigarette butt?" he reiterated.

That was the moment my inner volcano erupted. "Screw it," I declared, grabbing my keys and dropping them on a table. "On Friday night, I had a .45 with a silencer pressed to my head. I should be in Florence, Italy, guiding tourists along the Arno River and showing them Michelangelo's David. What am I doing here in Goodlettsville, Tennessee, in the middle of nowhere, listening to country music while someone tried to shoot me? And you're asking about a cigarette butt on a mantel? You have the keys. I'm leaving."

As I turned to leave, George recognized he had gone too far. He did not offer counseling or check on my well-being. However, he did apologize and expressed respect for my work ethic and leadership. He then left without mentioning the cigarette butt again.

George was terrible with people; interacting with him was like dealing with a Dictator, and he had a fierce temper (you could see his jugular vein bulging when he got worked up). But he was deeply committed to quality.

Two weeks after our confrontation, he promoted me to general manager. He asked me to run one of his restaurants in New Orleans, a city I had not visited since staying with my father nearly a dozen years earlier. I accepted George's offer.

I was off on another adventure that would change my life and leave a lasting impact on the restaurant industry worldwide. It was during this journey that I created the famous Bloomin' Onion.

Ten

Becoming a Flavorist

Over the years, many people have described me as a "chef."

I am not.

I have been around many talented chefs over the years, dating back to Michel Poumay in Aspen. Michel spent years studying culinary arts at the École Hôtellière de Liège in Belgium, mastering techniques and traditions of European cuisine.

I did none of that.

My talent is not in cooking or leading a kitchen brigade. My gift is understanding raw ingredients, their chemistry, quirks, and hidden potential, and preparing them in ways that make foods people crave. The chefs of the Crescent City taught me everything I know about seasonings and spices that later helped make Outback Steakhouse a success.

I am a flavorist, not a chef.

Warren Leruth embodied both roles: a chef and a flavorist, a rare combination. I met him at LeRuth's, his renowned five-star restaurant on Franklin Street in Gretna, on the West Bank of New Orleans. Warren was instrumental in igniting a renaissance in New Orleans cuisine.

Warren, once a physics student, became an expert in authentic taste and flavor. In 1965, he started LeRuth's, a restaurant whose capital "R" stood for the restaurant, not himself. Before he arrived, many New Orleans eateries used repetitive menus with familiar dishes. By skillfully combining classic French techniques with traditional New Orleans cuisine, Warren changed the city's dining scene and encouraged a new wave of chefs to explore broader culinary options and innovate.

Warren was especially famous for two inventions: his oyster-artichoke soup and sautéed soft-shell crab with lump crab meat. He baked his own bread and crafted desserts, including ice cream, something rare at the time. One critic called his restaurant "a culinary miracle ... one of the finest eating places in the world." Word spread quickly about Warren's skills, and by the mid-1970s, celebrities such as Yul Brynner, Walter Cronkite, and Charles Kuralt were making reservations months in advance.

Once, Warren competed against the renowned Paul Bocuse in a culinary contest. Bocuse, celebrated as the father of nouvelle cuisine, was the favorite to win. Nevertheless, Warren won the grand prize, marking one of the most memorable moments of his illustrious career.

With Chef Paul Bocuse, New Orleans.

I first went to LeRuth's in 1975 with George Biel and my supervisor, Gary Link. George had hired me at the Steak and Ale in New Orleans. He was well known in the culinary world. He started as a waiter at Steak and Ale, where Norman Brinker hired him, and was later promoted to a supervisor overseeing the flagship location on Lemmon Avenue in Dallas.

The food at LeRuth's was extraordinary in that tiny Victorian house in Gretna, on the West Bank of New Orleans, where Warren had converted it into a restaurant. I was so blown away by the flavors that I can still remember the menu almost exactly: trout amandine, oysters Bienville, avocado tropique salad, rack of lamb, lobster wrapped in trout, and Warren's famous Coquilles Saint-Jacques, a seafood dish crusted in a shell and baked in the oven.

After a few bites, George and I were amazed by Warren's culinary talent. We quickly agreed that his cooking was aspirational, the kind we aspired to master someday. At one point, Warren came to our table, recognizing our enthusiasm for the industry and our understanding of food and flavor, and invited us to his home that very night.

I still remember what he served us, as if I had just tasted it moments ago: an exceptional Mumm Champagne named after the company's president, René Lalou, a close friend of Warren's. As we sat in Warren's living room, we discussed every aspect of food late into the night: quality, excellent ingredients, different dishes, and combinations. It felt less like a casual chat and more like a master class. We finally left a little after four in the morning, our minds buzzing with ideas.

But something else happened at that dinner that I have never forgotten.

I looked at George and said, "George, we should be serving this kind of food in casual dining. This is what casual dining needs."

He agreed with me.

At that time, food like this was reserved for the wealthy, special occasions, and people who could afford fine dining. The average family going out to dinner could never experience flavors like these at a restaurant. That did not seem right to us. Why should a beautiful meal out be a privilege? Why should great restaurant food belong only to a few?

That dinner at LeRuth's planted a seed. Chef-inspired food belongs in casual dining, priced affordably. Everyone deserves a seat at the table. Everyone should have access to a beautiful dinner at an affordable price with great service. That vision began at Warren's table and would drive everything I did from that moment forward.

After that night, Warren became a great mentor, and his guidance would prove essential in the years ahead.

When Warren passed away at age seventy-two in 2001, I chose to celebrate his legendary talents. I arranged a culinary tribute featuring his most famous dishes. We paid homage to his genius with Potage LeRuth, the oyster-artichoke soup he created, and Crabmeat St. Frances, a baked ramekin of crabmeat with pepper sauce. We ended with his rich dessert, Macaroon Bread Pudding. It was a meaningful tribute to a truly unique individual.

For over three hours, on the side of the church under elm trees, 300 of us wined and dined and told stories about the life and legacy of Warren Leruth.

Warren would have been proud to see his life honored while his friends shared stories of how he helped many of us. We enjoyed French wines, including René Lalou Champagne, and savored Warren's finest dishes and private recipes.

After Warren's tribute, I was ready to spread my wings and enter the restaurant industry on my own.

After several years working with Steak & Ale in New Orleans, I chose to become an independent restaurateur. I have never shied away from risks; from sneaking out my mom's car window at age three, to the trip to El Paso as a teen, to journeys to Italy and across Europe as a college sophomore. Now, I am ready to do what I always do: bet on myself.

New Orleans was one of the few markets in the country where chefs owned and managed their own restaurants. At that time, the most famous chef in America was Paul Prudhomme of K-Paul's Louisiana Kitchen. Paul's success story was enlightening to me and, in a way, provided a roadmap I would later follow.

Paul was renowned for his blackened redfish, which became very popular. It was even selected as an entrée at the 1983 Williamsburg Economic Summit. The famous Craig Claiborne, who curated the All-American menu, chose Paul's blackened redfish "to add a touch of elegance" to the meal and, of course, to ensure it was full of flavor.

Most people did not realize that redfish was not very popular before Paul started serving it at his restaurant. It is a game fish thriving in the Atlantic Ocean and the Gulf of Mexico, but back then, on the plate, it was often considered bland and unremarkable. Many diners viewed it as a filler fish lacking distinction. However, Paul saw potential where others saw mediocrity. Through persistent trial and error, he discovered how to make it flavorful, effectively creating his own signature.

Paul's first step was unexpectedly simple: coat a redfish fillet with butter and a mixture of seventeen spices. He then seared it in a hot black skillet for about ninety seconds on each side. His method involved high-temperature searing, which is almost reckless. If you try to replicate Paul's blackened redfish at home, your fire alarm will most likely go off. Believe me. This highlights one of the key benefits of using a commercial hood vent.

No one had ever tasted anything like Paul's blackened redfish. The secret was the white-hot skillet that fused his seventeen-spice blend into new flavors. While others used cayenne, oregano, thyme, and similar herbs, they did not combine them at such high heat. This intense heat altered the spices' chemistry, revealing unique notes and aromas never before experienced. What started as a simple fish was transformed into something extraordinary and unforgettable.

People could not get enough of his redfish, even if it looked burnt. The char was part of the magic. Simply put, there was a thrill to it, a sensory jolt that people felt the moment they tasted it. It had what we call "New Orleans comeback flavor," a flavor so compelling it pulls you back to the restaurant again and again. And this is precisely what I became adept at: identifying those flavors and presenting them to eager customers.

Again, I was not a chef. I had no formal culinary training. I did not spend decades in kitchens across the country as a sous chef, learning the tricks of the trade. Flavor became my focus, my North Star, my obsession. It became the skill that set me apart from others in my field.

Paul Prudhomme was a pioneer. Soon after his blackened redfish became the talk of the New Orleans restaurant scene, local chefs began crafting bold flavors in small restaurants. The city buzzed with experimentation, each kitchen pushing boundaries and each chef chasing that elusive signature flavor.

That wave of innovation motivated me to leave Steak and Ale and start my own path.

My first independent project was managing Stephen & Martin's, which I revamped into New Orleans' first gourmet Creole bistro. I brought in Jalla St. James, a Creole chef who served as a minister on

Sundays and did his own kind of divine work in my kitchen during the week. He prepared all the traditional Creole dishes with both respect and creativity. His red beans and rice were unmatched. Why? Because he truly understood flavor and knew how to draw out depth in simple ingredients, allowing a humble dish to shine.

Stephen and Martin's, New Orleans.

My next venture, Bouligny, quickly established itself as the top Creole bistro in New Orleans. I brought on Chef Sebastian "Buster" Ambrosia to oversee the kitchen in a refurbished firehouse at the corner of Magazine and Marengo.

From opening night, Bouligny was an immediate success. Our casual menu included delicious options like oysters bonne femme and grilled duck breast, and the vibe was warm, energetic, and truly New Orleans. However, despite its popularity, my partners and I did not work well together. While personality clashes are common across industries, they can be particularly damaging in restaurants. I needed to find a way to exit.

As it turned out, someone had been watching my career since my days at Stephen & Martin's: Al Copeland.

Al was a New Orleans original. Born in the St. Thomas housing project, he dropped out of high school at sixteen and worked as a soda jerk before buying a donut shop from his brother. In 1972, he opened Popeyes Chicken & Biscuits, and it took off. By the early 1980s, Popeyes had that unmistakable New Orleans comeback flavor, and Al had hundreds of locations. He was famous around New Orleans for Popeyes, his speedboats, and his elaborate Christmas light displays, which caused traffic jams throughout the neighborhood.

But Al wanted more. In 1983, he opened Copeland's of New Orleans, a sit-down restaurant specializing in Cajun and Creole cuisine. His vision was to bring New Orleans' greatest chefs under one roof, serving dishes like blackened redfish, roast Cajun duck, and coconut beer-battered shrimp, all for under ten dollars. This was his move into fine dining, and he needed someone who understood flavor. He hired me as an executive.

Working for Al was great. It provided me with a steady job and a backup salary while I continued searching for my next entrepreneurial adventure.

I discovered it in New Orleans' neglected warehouse district. It was the first time in a century that the World's Fair had come to the Crescent City. Based on what I had seen at the 1966 World's Fair in New York, I expected huge, hungry crowds. Al agreed to let me pursue it as a side project while I continued working for him.

Seizing this rare opportunity, I decided to take action. I reached out to my friend Pete Fountain, a renowned jazz clarinetist. Pete's path into jazz was quite intriguing. He was born to a truck driver on White Street in New Orleans. As a child, Pete was fragile and often suffered from respiratory infections because of his weak lungs. During a visit to the pharmacy, Pete's father discussed his son's health with a local doctor. The following day, the doctor examined Pete and recommended an unusual treatment: introducing a musical instrument for him to blow into.

Pete's father took him to a musical instrument store right away. At first, Pete wanted the drums, but that did not meet the doctor's recommendation. Next, he chose the clarinet. Once they were home, Pete could not produce any sound; the instrument was too challenging for his weak lungs. But over time, as his lungs strengthened from blowing, Pete began making music. The clarinet became his salvation, his therapy, and ultimately his voice. By the time I met him, Pete was famous for his solo performances on ABC's The Lawrence

Welk Show and for leading his own band in French Quarter clubs.

Early in our friendship, I asked Pete a surprising question: "Does water still spit out of a clarinet into your backyard pool?"

"How do you know what my pool looks like?" he replied.

"Because I built it," I said. "I was on the Flamingo Pools crew that built your pool."

Just mentioning the name, Flamingo Pools, flooded my mind with painful memories. I instantly thought of my father: his detachment, his disregard for others, and the sense that he did not care about me.

But I also remembered my co-workers, the kindness they showed me by sharing their food, and the words they spoke that stayed with me: that a better life awaited me and that I should not be stuck in those pits forever. It all came rushing back to me as I talked with Pete about his pool.

In many ways, I took those words to heart. I built a better life for myself, leaving behind those overheated holes. Looking back, I have already achieved far more than I thought possible while working alongside them that summer. If only I could find those friends now, I would thank them from the bottom of my heart for giving me hope and inspiring me to reach for something better.

Pete was surprised that I helped construct his pool, which brought us closer. We planned to start a business before the World's Fair began. We rented a 2,000-seat space in a large warehouse at St. Joseph and Fulton Streets, calling it "Pete Fountain's Reunion Hall." It was perfect for a jazz venue, with high visibility on the World's Fair midway and an embodiment of New Orleans' spirit.

But then I walked into the kitchen, and my whole outlook on the place shifted.

"You have got to be kidding me!" I said aloud.

I had seen larger kitchens in a 100-seat restaurant. But what other choice did I have? None. This was going to be my kitchen, whether I liked it or not, so I got to work. That moment highlighted a vital part of my philosophy: I never blamed others when I faced challenging situations. Complaining does not fix problems. I would keep my head down, stay quiet, and focus on what needed to be done. What is the point of griping and whining about something you cannot change? There is none. It is a waste of oxygen and time, and it will not earn you any friends among coworkers.

I assembled a staff, created the menu, and started testing recipes for a commercial kitchen, not a gourmet bistro. Instead of sauté pans and stew pots, we used sixty-gallon kettles to prepare classic New Orleans dishes.

The deal I negotiated gave the venue fifty percent of every food dollar I earned. In return, I had to provide all the equipment myself. It was a steep price, but I believed in the opportunity.

Equipment was the largest capital expense. I brought in George Zisis, a restaurant equipment dealer, as my partner. George could obtain commercial-grade equipment at the manufacturer's price. We purchased steel-jacketed steam kettles, the best on the market. We had four sixty-gallon kettles for soups and two large skillet pans for jambalaya.

George provided the equipment. I had to provide the funds.

I went to Hibernia Bank and met Tommy Westervelt, a blue-blooded uptown New Orleans gentleman who had become one of my customers. He believed in me. He gave me a signature loan for $250,000. A signature loan meant I had no assets to cover the collateral. It was based entirely on trust.

I told Tommy, "I appreciate this. It is the first time a banker has really believed in me. I have no assets to cover the collateral."

He looked at me and said, "Just don't default on me. Don't make me look bad."

I never forgot those words. Even in the hardest times, when I started at Outback on a $50,000 salary and still owed hundreds of thousands from the World's Fair failure, it never occurred to me not to make those payments. Tommy trusted me, and I would honor that trust.

By the time the World's Fair opened on May 12, 1984, my menu included red beans and rice, gumbo, jambalaya, crawfish étouffée, shrimp étouffée, and, of course, bread pudding. From the start, we were feeding ten thousand people a day. We had hit the jackpot!

Pete was at the peak of his career, widely acclaimed for his talent. He frequently appeared on The Lawrence Welk Show and on The Tonight Show with Johnny Carson. As America's most famous clarinetist and a globally recognized artist, he attracted large crowds. The Neville Brothers often showed up unexpectedly to add their unique sound, enhancing the atmosphere. By combining Pete's music with my food sales, we achieved significant nightly profits and provided a fantastic experience. I truly enjoyed being an entrepreneur when money was flowing into our accounts.

Cooking jambalaya at the food trial for the 1984 World's Fair, which led to the chef role at Pete Fountain's Reunion Hall.

I also learned a lot during that time. For example, we had to cook all 10,000 meals the day before, chill them, then reheat and serve. The biggest challenge was chilling the food quickly enough. Seafood is delicate and picks up bacteria quickly, so it had to be chilled immediately.

To find a solution, I contacted a Cargill employee who helped Popeyes with their chilling systems. He said he could install a cook-chill system for $500,000. I told him I did not have that kind of money and was opening next week. He said there was another way. We purchased brand-new, large garbage cans, cleaned and lined them, and filled them with ice. He showed me how to seal the food in plastic bags and drop them into the ice bath. The direct contact chilled the food as quickly as any other system. That was how we solved it.

For three months, we performed well, serving ten thousand people daily. I enlisted some of New Orleans' top chefs to assist us. Industry experts recognized the difficulties of operating in such a confined space, yet we still managed to create outstanding dishes despite these constraints.

However, my feelings quickly shifted from affection to loathing.

None of us had anticipated the significant decline in attendance at the World's Fair that summer. Several factors could explain this. Some believed that the 1984 Summer Olympics in Los Angeles, which drew millions to Southern California, might have diverted visitors. Others noted that the fair occurred just two years later and only two states away from Knoxville's 1982 World Fair. Additionally, some argued that Walt Disney's EPCOT Center, opened in 1982, drew visitors to Orlando instead. To make matters worse, the organizers failed to attract any major exhibitors.

Then came the bad press. The Wall Street Journal and others said it was not a real World's Fair; it was a fake. We quickly went from ten thousand people a day to eight hundred, almost overnight.

I recall a Newsweek reporter visiting to interview me. He had prepared the complete story of the World's Fair and the elegance of Reunion Hall, ready for publication. As we toured the Fair together, he suddenly fainted and passed away. He experienced a cardiac arrest right in my arms. I liked him and admired the story he had written. That Newsweek article would have greatly benefited us, but it was never published.

To this day, the 1984 World's Fair remains the only exposition to declare bankruptcy during its run, and it is no coincidence that since then, there has not been another in the United States. For me, it was a financial disaster, a failed investment that haunted me for many years. My name was on contracts for hundreds of thousands of dollars' worth of equipment and leases.

Although the World's Fair was a big letdown, many still appreciated and praised the food from my kitchen. Industry experts understood the challenges of working in such a small space, yet we managed to produce exceptional dishes despite those limitations.

Alvin Copeland was born in New Orleans and raised by his mother in the St. Thomas public housing project after his father left the family shortly after his birth. At sixteen, he dropped out of high school and went to work as a soda jerk at Schwegmann Brothers Giant Supermarket in Gentilly, serving sodas, milkshakes, and ice cream drinks at a counter that resembled an old-fashioned drugstore.

Later, Al worked at Tastee Donut, a chain partly owned by his brother Gil. At eighteen, he sold his car to buy a donut shop from his brother, launching his career as a restaurant and franchise owner.

While still in his twenties, Al opened a chicken shack called Chicken on the Run, specializing in Southern fried chicken. But he faced a formidable competitor: Kentucky Fried Chicken was thriving with tens of thousands of locations nationwide, including more than a dozen in the greater New Orleans area alone. Chicken on the Run did not last long.

Undeterred by failure, a common experience among those who achieve their goals, Al kept working, hustling, and thinking about how to succeed in the business. After closing Chicken on the Run, he launched a new venture, removing fried chicken from the menu and naming it Popeye's Chicken & Biscuits. Soon after opening, lines of customers wrapped around the block. Why? Popeye's brought the unmistakable New Orleans comeback flavor. In that moment, Al found his Velcro.

And this was before Warren Leruth created the world's best buttermilk biscuit for Al to add to the menu. When Warren's biscuit debuted in 1983, it became an instant hit, turning Al into a millionaire almost overnight.

As the chaos of the 1984 World's Fair subsided, Al decided to open an upscale restaurant named Copeland's of New Orleans. Thanks to the success of many Popeyes locations, he had the funds to support this new venture. Unlike fast-food outlets, Copeland's is a sit-down restaurant that focuses on New Orleans cuisine and remains so today. Why did Al pursue this? Having built his reputation in fast food, he, like many ambitious entrepreneurs, was eager to expand into more refined dining and enhance his status in the restaurant industry.

This is why he asked me to oversee research and development in his company's kitchen. He offered an unlimited budget, which was extremely tempting. I accepted right away. Having recently married and become a father of two, I was also responsible for unpaid bills from the World's Fair worth hundreds of thousands of dollars. It was clear I desperately needed funds and had no options left.

After several years working in the trenches at Stephen & Martin's, Bouligny, and Pete Fountain's Reunion Hall, I was finally calling the shots in my own research kitchen, my own food laboratory. Al wanted Copeland's to succeed, and he fully supported me, giving me the freedom to explore the New Orleans dining scene and then return to the test kitchen to experiment with versions of recipes that intrigued me.

I had always been motivated to unlock the secrets of spices and temperatures, but working for Al and testing concepts and ideas in my personal laboratory was when I truly became a flavorist. I was constantly searching for new ideas and flavor combinations in New Orleans. The entire city became my test kitchen, my blank canvas where I was free to use any brushstrokes I wanted to create my own version of flavorist art.

During the day, I worked one-on-one with our chefs in Copeland's test kitchen. At night, I explored the city in search of new foods and flavors. My goal was to try as many different dishes as possible at the hundreds of restaurants that made New Orleans the nation's culinary capital. Each night, I never knew what to expect. Every night was a new adventure.

And then, on an ordinary evening when I did not expect to find anything unusual, it happened:

I discovered my Velcro!

Eleven

The Game Changer – The Onion Mum

The day in 1984 when everything changed is etched in my memory as clearly as the birth of my children.

I had spent the afternoon in Copeland's test kitchen, working through a new batch of ideas. By evening, I was restless. That was normal. Most nights, I drove across New Orleans, visiting restaurants, tasting dishes, and studying what other chefs were doing. Paul Prudhomme and Warren Leruth were introducing food that most Americans had never seen before, and their creativity pushed me to explore the limits of what I could achieve, not as a chef but as a flavorist.

In New Orleans in the mid-1980s, such exploration was welcome. Chefs shared ideas freely. You could walk into another man's kitchen, taste his latest creation, tell him the seasoning was off, and he would thank you for it. Collaboration was not a threat. It was how we all got better.

That evening, I drove to Russell Cuoco's restaurant on Pontchartrain Boulevard, a small place by the lake with maybe sixty seats. Russell's Marine and Grill had been open only a few years, but it had already built a loyal following, and the reason was Jeff Glowski.

Jeff was an exceptionally talented chef and a genuinely good person, the kind of individual you would want on your team. He managed a bustling kitchen that served breakfast, lunch, and dinner, with constant prepping, staffing, and sourcing. To outsiders, the rhythm appeared chaotic, like scattered marbles on a concrete floor. Yet Jeff kept everything under control. He was careful, organized, and skilled at creating dishes that made customers eager to return.

That evening, I entered into the restaurant alone and sat at a table. Outside, the Louisiana sun was setting, its rays reflecting off the water like sparkling diamonds. A refreshing breeze blew through the trees.

I was enjoying the view when Jeff began sending plates to my table, eager to show me his latest dishes and get my feedback.

First came a steaming batch of fried oysters. They were delicious. Moments later, Jeff hurried out of the kitchen, always busy and juggling many tasks, and quickly approached my table. After a short hello, he explained how he was battering the oysters differently and what new spices he had added. I shared my thoughts, noting what worked and what could be improved. I even suggested he try a dish I recently tasted at Uglesich's, hoping it might inspire something new.

Jeff then told me not to move, claiming he had something that would blow my mind and hurried back to the kitchen. He returned with a game-changing, career-changing, life-changing item: a golden, fragrant, deep-fried onion that looked more like a flower than a vegetable.

As a flavorist and foodie, I found the presentation to be purely sensual, engaging every sense to the fullest.

In an instant, I realized this was what I had been searching for since that summer at Twin Farms in El Paso, Texas.

It was my Velcro.

Jeff called his creation the Onion Mum. I had never seen anything like it. The most intriguing aspect was its appearance: layers of onion, hand-cut to resemble a flower's petals. That was how you ate it: you plucked a petal, dunked it in dipping sauce, and popped it into your mouth. Even before tasting it, I stared at the appetizer for what felt like ten minutes, with one thought running through my mind: This is the dish that will put me on the Polo field.

Finally, I asked Jeff, "How did you...?"

Jeff laughed. "Pretty wild, isn't it?" he said. "I got the idea from a book called Japanese Garnishes."

Over the centuries, the Japanese had developed a specialized art form called mukimono. Think of it as carving a Halloween pumpkin, only more elaborate. The creations were stunning: a tulip carved from a tomato, an apple shaped into a bunny, a radish transformed into a blooming rose. Mukimono was not about taste; its only goal was beauty, creating garnishes that caught the eye.

Tucked away on one of the last pages of Japanese Garnishes was the Onion Flower. Jeff, with his keen instincts, spotted it and believed it belonged not on a buffet table as decoration but on a dinner menu as an appetizer.

Let us pause and savor this moment. As I gaze at this beautiful, vibrant Onion Mum, a realization strikes me: life can change unexpectedly, and fate can grant you the very thing you have dreamed of for years when you least expect it.

But here's the truth: I was prepared for this moment.

It all began almost twenty years earlier, on Bud Heatley's ranch in Texas, when he gave me that memorable speech about discovering my Velcro.

My thoughts drifted back to El Paso. I remember being a skinny, anxious, introverted fifteen-year-old with no clear goals. Back then, I was going through the motions of life, like a robot stuck in a routine. I was not living to my full potential.

It was then that Bud offered his advice, and his words profoundly shaped my life. I vividly remember asking him, "Why didn't somebody else invent Velcro?"

Now, sitting at Russell Cuoco's restaurant, still admiring the Onion Mum, my Velcro is right in front of me. And as I look at it, I can almost hear Bud's voice answering that question.

"Think about it," Bud had said. "How many of us have the training to analyze something as microscopic as a burr the way De Mestral did? Or the tools he had at his disposal, the delicate instruments that could surgically assemble a small loop with a hook? And what about the patience and persistence that Velcro demanded? How many of your friends would be willing to spend a decade on an idea that may or may not even have any marketable value?"

His words echoed in my mind. I had not planned it this way, but I had done precisely what Bud advised: I spent decades, armed with patience and persistence, searching for an idea that could succeed in a vast marketplace.

I trained for this moment, learning the nuances of the restaurant business, the intricacies of flavor, the desires of customers, and what truly appeals to a worldwide audience. Simply put, I was prepared; I had spent almost my entire adult life getting ready for this.

I kept replaying Bud's words in my mind, each delivered with that Texas twang. I felt as if Bud was sitting right beside me, smiling and shouting at the top of his lungs: This is your Velcro! This is your God-damn Velcro!

All of this took only seconds, but to me it felt like hours. I was swept up in a memory, the echo of Bud's voice and the words that changed the course of my life. His wisdom lingered in the air, wrapping around me and pulling me deeper into reflection. For a moment, time stood still. Then, with a conscious effort, I shook off the reverie and returned to the present, the precious present, the place I always strive to inhabit.

Grounded once more, I reached out and gently plucked a single petal from the Onion Mum. I dipped it delicately into the rich, fragrant sauce and brought it to my lips. As I tasted it, a burst of flavor filled my mouth, an explosion of savory, succulent delight.

The onion's petals, soft and yielding, seemed to dissolve as I chewed, each bite igniting my senses. My mind, awakened by the taste, began to race with ideas: new spices, unexpected pairings, ways to elevate this humble onion into an appetizer that would captivate the masses. The flavorist in me kicked into overdrive. My mind whirred with ideas, spices, and techniques I wanted to test.

"Tone down the black pepper and add some more cayenne," I told Jeff, who was watching me with wide eyes, recognizing my excitement. "Is this the right onion? It could be a tad sweeter. What about the batter? How long did they soak this?"

In specific industries, questions like these might have been viewed as demeaning or insensitive. But in the New Orleans restaurant scene of the mid-1980s, collaboration and honest feedback were essential for progress. We valued open exchange of ideas, and debate was not a threat but a catalyst for the gradual development of new dishes. By continually pushing each other to improve our skills, we became better chefs, our restaurant grew stronger, and our customers left happier.

Jeff expected genuine feedback. We both knew this was a rare creation with the potential to be perfect. Perfection required conversation, trial, and refinement, one idea at a time, one taste at a time.

Still seated and amazed, I reflected on Warren Leruth. His Coquilles St. Jacques was among the few dishes I regarded as perfect, and altering it felt almost sacrilegious. Jeff's Onion Mum was not quite perfect yet, but I believed it could reach that level with more time, effort, and long hours in the test kitchen.

Within moments, I envisioned the dozens of steps required to bring this dish to life. This appetizer had the potential to transform everything for my family and me, and could even change how people worldwide viewed onions and their flavor.

After talking more with Jeff and taking a few more bites of the Onion Mum, I finally left the restaurant. Darkness had fallen over the town. My instincts urged me to go back to Copeland's test kitchen right away, but my mind told me to rest and approach my dream fresh in the morning.

Before sunrise, I was already in Copeland's test kitchen. I took Jeff's idea and made small tweaks, adjusting each element carefully. After months of working long hours to perfect the flavor and texture, I finally added it to Copeland's menu, transforming the restaurant into my live testing space. I watched how customers reacted, walking the floor, greeting guests, but mainly observing their faces for signs of satisfaction, happiness, and eagerness for more; these are the clearest indicators of success in the restaurant industry.

One evening, about two years later, my best friend from my Steak and Ale days walked through the door. Chris Sullivan had flown in from Tampa to attend the 1987 Final Four at the Superdome. By then, Chris, like me, had moved on from Steak and Ale. However, unlike me, Chris had achieved major success.

After leaving Steak and Ale, Chris became a joint venture partner and franchisee with Norman Brinker at Chili's. Alongside Bob Basham and Trudy Cooper, he absolutely nailed that deal; we are talking a Babe Ruth moonshot.

Over the next three years, they launched seventeen Chili's outlets throughout Florida, expanding swiftly like pioneers during a gold rush. Norman, the ever-supportive mentor, was delighted and sold his share to the trio. Although Bob and Trudy remained involved for some time, Chris, driven by his entrepreneurial drive, was already chasing his next major project.

I was excited to see him. We shared old stories, and I guided him to our best table, offering a perfect view and cozy ambiance. I was eager to share my latest work. While I call it a "creation," Jeff Glowski truly deserves all the credit for inspiring the idea. My part was to refine and enhance it into the famous Bloomin' Onion.

Chris looked over the menu and complimented how I had put together the culinary puzzle. He enjoyed our hometown specialties:

Bayou Broccoli, Cajun Gumbo Ya Ya, Jambalaya Pasta, and Eggplant Pirogue. For years, he worked on Norman's ideas, designed to attract the widest audience. Steak and Ale's menus were simple, approachable, familiar, and safe. That was Norman's genius, which helped make Steak and Ale very successful.

But Chris wanted more. He craved a challenge for his palate, seeking tastes he had never encountered. That night, he relished the dishes I served, his mouth bursting with flavors he rarely experienced. Still, nothing could have prepared him for Copeland's take on the Onion Mum.

When I brought the plate to the table, his eyes widened at the sight of the Onion Mum. He said, "That's an incredible appetizer. Is that difficult to make?"

"It sure is," I replied. "It's an incredible pain in the ass!"

And it was. In all my years in the restaurant business, I had never encountered a more labor-intensive task. Each onion had to be peeled by hand, petal by petal, layer by layer. Once the outer petals were removed, the next layer had to be cut in an offset pattern to create the bloom. It was painstaking work.

We had one employee whose only job was to prepare onions all day, twenty-four petals per onion, before they were battered and fried. If the dish had been a $19.95 entrée, we would have made money easily. But at $3.95 as an appetizer, it was pure labor of love.

Sourcing the right onion was another challenge. I changed the onion to a Spanish colossal onion. I did this because it transmitted the spices and flavors better than the Vidalia onion that Jeff used.

The typical onion measures three inches across, yet our recipe called for one four and a quarter inches. That extra inch and a quarter was vital to the presentation. Diners were not accustomed to seeing onions that large, and their surprise heightened the experience. "Is that really an onion?" they would ask. However, finding onions of that size was very difficult. Still, I remained hopeful because the dish was too good to abandon.

I explained all this to Chris as he enjoyed his second bite. I can still see the satisfaction on his face. He kept talking about how much he loved it, calling it the best appetizer he had ever had. His enthusiasm meant a lot to me.

After a long night of eating and talking, we promised to keep in touch. Chris was already imagining his next idea, his mind always full of concepts, and he thought he might have something that would catch my interest.

I was intrigued, mainly because of the onion. I knew it would never work at Copeland's. The restaurant was too small. This appetizer required time, capital, and scale.

It needed to be featured on the menu of a national chain, a stage large enough to showcase its uniqueness. I believed with all my heart that this onion could be the cornerstone of a new chain, its face, the reason people came through the doors.

Some products endure for generations. George Smith's lollipop, created in 1908 and named after his favorite racehorse, is still with us today. I believed this onion could have that staying power.

Around the same time, Stuart Sargent was also considering a new restaurant. Stuart was one of the most talented restaurateurs of our generation. He had founded Studebaker's in 1980 and launched several successful club-entertainment ventures. He was the real deal.

I met Stuart through my childhood friend Phil Heatley, who by then had earned his law degree from the University of Texas and was working in Houston. Phil and Stuart were members of the Houston Polo Club, and once Phil introduced us, Stuart and I quickly became friends. We shared two passions, polo and restaurants, and could talk for hours about both. A few years later, we served as groomsmen together at Phil's wedding to Shelley Sachnik.

Stuart knew my track record when he reached out to me about developing a new concept. His idea was straightforward: create the best diner in America, with food and ambiance that would keep customers coming back. He believed loyal patrons came from satisfying food and atmosphere, not alcohol. He already had a location in San Antonio, the Uptown Diner, and he wanted me as a partner, not an employee. I was flattered.

Meanwhile, Chris Sullivan asked me to come to Tampa to collaborate with him and Bob Basham on their upcoming project. Although they specialized in steakhouses, they had no concept, brand, or venue. To make matters worse, the federal government had issued a health advisory encouraging Americans to reduce red meat intake and eat more poultry and fish. Considering all these factors, it is no surprise I declined Chris's invitation and opted for Stuart's.

I gave Al Copeland two weeks' notice, packed my belongings into boxes, and drove to San Antonio, believing I was on the threshold of a winner. Sadly, I only lasted two months. My final attempt in the Alamo City was brief.

To this day, Stuart and I have built the best diner in America. But there was one major flaw: the restaurant made no profit. The numbers told the story. On a Saturday, we served 1,000 meals. The cash in the till was $5,000. That averages out to five dollars per person, including tax. Uptown Diner did not make financial sense, and in the end, the diner did not last.

After six weeks, Stuart and I agreed to shut it down. When it was time to split the assets, Stuart was a gentleman. He handed me a severance check, which I desperately needed. I still owed money from the 1984 World's Fair failure, worsened by double-digit interest rates. My finances looked more like a Pollock painting than a Picasso, chaotic, splattered, and messy.

Not knowing where else to turn after Uptown Diner collapsed, I did what I had often done before: I relied on my best friend, Phil Heatley. Unfortunately, I was going through a divorce. Feeling depressed and lost, I packed my life into my car once again and drove to Phil's house in Houston.

I was in a deep funk. I had risked everything on Uptown Diner and come up short again. For me, this was the New Orleans World's Fair, Part II. After the World's Fair, I had gone to work for Al Copeland. Now I had nothing. No job. No safety net. No Plan B.

At Phil's house, I slept on the couch and stared at the ceiling fan for hours, watching it turn in the same slow circles while my mind refused to stop. Phil gave me space, but I could feel his concern. The debt sat on me like a physical weight: over $200,000 at double-digit interest rates. Some nights, the numbers ran through my head whether I wanted them to or not. At 18 percent, my debt was growing by more than a hundred dollars a day. I was getting poorer in my sleep.

The questions came in waves, always worse in the small hours of the morning. Should I stay in Texas? Should I go back to New Orleans? Should I give up the restaurant business altogether? I had been in this industry for fifteen years and had almost nothing to show for it.

Then, in the quiet of one of those sleepless nights, a thought cut through the noise: the fried onion. I still had the recipe I had perfected at Copeland's, and I still had Chris Sullivan's phone number.

I did not call right away. I kept rehearsing what I would say, then put the phone down. The last time Chris made that offer, I was running research and development at Copeland's, backed by an unlimited budget and a team of the best chefs in New Orleans. Now I was sleeping on my best friend's couch. I fully expected him to modify the deal, offering less equity, different terms, or saying the window had closed.

When I finally dialed, the house was quiet. I sat in Phil's kitchen, receiver in hand, and listened to the phone ring.

Chris picked up, and the warmth in his voice was immediate. I told him the truth. I told him about the diner, how Stuart and I had built something beautiful that could not turn a profit, and how a thousand customers a day at five dollars a head was a recipe for bankruptcy. Chris laughed at that. He had the kind of laugh that made you feel like your failures were just good stories waiting for a better ending.

Then the laughter faded, and I forced myself to ask the question I had been rehearsing.

"Chris, is the equity position you offered me still on the table?"

The pause could not have lasted more than a second. It felt much longer.

"Of course it is," he said. "Nothing has changed."

"The same terms?"

"Same equity. Same terms. Same deal."

He said it as if the idea of changing the terms had never occurred to him. I had spent days dreading this call, while Chris Sullivan had not spent two seconds reconsidering his word.

I stood up from the kitchen table. My hands were shaking, but not from fear anymore. In a single conversation, the weight I had been carrying for months did not disappear, but it shifted. For the first time since the diner collapsed, I could see a way forward.

That single gesture told me everything I needed to know about Chris Sullivan. He did not see a desperate man calling from a friend's kitchen. He saw a partner. His integrity and his trust in me at my lowest point were worth more than any number on a check.

Before I accepted, I went to see my good friend Al Copeland to let him know what I was doing. I was also curious about what Al might say.

Al knew what I was worth to him. I was his link to every great chef in New Orleans. I was the recruiter who walked into Ruth's Chris Steak House, Antoine's, Galatoire's, and Commander's Palace and convinced their chefs to join Al's test kitchen. One after another, I brought them in. And one after another, we created priceless recipes. Onion Mum. The popcorn shrimp. The broccoli cheese balls. Blackened redfish. Roast Cajun duck. Al knew that talent like mine did not come along often.

When I told Al I was leaving, he became upset. "Why are you leaving?" he asked.

"They're offering me equity," I replied.

Al did not believe in giving away ownership. He never had. But he also knew how desperate I was. He knew about the World's Fair debt and the 18% interest strangling me. So he tried to buy my allegiance.

He pulled out his checkbook, signed a blank check, and slid it across the desk. "Here," he said. "As long as it doesn't go over a million dollars."

This was 1987. A million dollars then would be worth several million today.

I took the check and walked to a corner of the room. For twenty minutes, I stared at it. I considered all the possibilities. The Hibernia loan: gone. The IRS debt: settled. I pictured my children, Chris and Kathleen, in a house with a real yard, not of another rented apartment. I pictured sleeping through a whole night without the interest ticking in my head.

Then I thought about Tampa. A restaurant that did not yet exist. A name nobody had chosen. Partners I trusted but with whom I had never built anything. Al's money would buy me relief. Chris's offer would make me a partner. And there was the difference. Al wanted to pay for my talent. Chris wanted to share a future.

I already knew my answer. I had always wanted to make my money WITH someone, not FOR someone.

I walked back, tore up the blank check, and returned the pieces to Al. "That's not how I want to earn my money," I said. "I want to earn it with someone, not for someone."

Al was upset. He knew what he was losing. He knew his money

had not worked. He told me I was making a mistake, that I would be back at his doorstep when whatever venture I chose failed.

Still, I knew something Al did not. His vision for casual dining was limited to twenty or thirty restaurants. I had dreams of four hundred, five hundred. And I knew that could only happen with partners who understood the power of sharing equity.

Tearing up that million-dollar check was the bravest thing I have ever done, finding the strength to destroy something I desperately needed because I sought something more.

Al told me I would regret it. Years later, he admitted he was wrong. We became friends again, and he even invited me to ride on his Mardi Gras float. But that reconciliation lay far in the future.

After I decided to tear up the million-dollar check, I called Chris back.

I asked, "Is your offer still open?"

"It sure is," he replied. "See you in Tampa."

"Great!" I said, hanging up the phone, feeling exhilarated. I had just been given not a second chance but a third.

While down on my luck and bills still piling up, I thought this was my final opportunity to succeed in the restaurant industry.

Still, I was a realist. I carried lingering anxiety from my recent failures. Yet I had complete confidence in Chris. He had a proven track record. He knew how to navigate the turbulent waters every new venture faces. He was detail-oriented, intuitive, and a master problem-solver. More than that, he understood people well. He could assess someone's skills faster than anyone I knew and place them in the perfect role to succeed. In the business world, Chris inspired confidence in everyone around him, especially me.

After I signed on with Chris and Bob for this new project, I kept asking myself: What had I done to deserve such a wonderful friend?

Joe Kadow, who later became a very good friend of mine, was the lawyer handling the contract and insisted I pay $10,000 to become a founding partner of the restaurant we would call Outback Steakhouse, money I did not have. Without a moment's hesitation, Chris wrote the check himself. No obligation. No conditions. He just had a belief in me, pure and simple.

That is when my confidence truly soared.

After accepting Chris's offer, I had to figure out how to get to

Tampa. I had spent every cent of the severance check Stuart gave me on bills. I could not sell my Acura; I needed a car, and the only valuable possession I had left was the Stalker Nafey polo saddle Bud Heatley gave me twenty years earlier.

Polo was still my dream, my motivation to earn money. But the dream was slipping away. I was thirty-nine, broke, with over $200,000 in debt and interest rates near twenty percent. I had two young children to support. Too many nights, my sleep was troubled by nightmares of bankruptcy and the fear of being labeled a failure.

That saddle meant everything to me. It symbolized my polo dreams. As long as I had it, I believed I could one day become a polo player. To my friends, it sounded far-fetched. How could a middle-aged man with no money become a world-class player in a sport that required millions? But to me, the saddle was hope. It was proof that dreams could still be chased.

With a heavy heart, I took my saddle to the Houston Polo Club and, reluctantly, asked if anyone wanted to buy it. A member named Bill Lund offered me $250. Like it or not, and I definitely did not like it, I had to accept. I handed him the saddle, in fear that I would never see that beautiful saddle again.

The next day, with my wallet full of cash, I threw my belongings into the trunk of my Acura Integra, merged onto the Eastex Freeway, and hit the gas.

My next big adventure, another one that would completely change my life, was about to begin.

Twelve

A Team Forms – And So Does a Name

Driving across the wide flats of Texas, past tumbleweeds and oil wells, I felt energized once more. The thrill of adventure always lifts my spirits, filling me with anticipation for the unknown joys, triumphs, and challenges that lie ahead.

Ever since my first trip to El Paso with my buddy Phil Heatley at age fifteen, I have suffered from a strong case of wanderlust, a relentless urge to explore new places, meet new people, and face new challenges. Change has never scared me. Taking chances has never intimidated me. Now, I was ready to embrace whatever lay ahead as I prepared to start the next chapter of my life.

I left Phil's house in Houston a few days before Thanksgiving. Instead of driving directly to Tampa to meet my new partners, Chris Sullivan and Bob Basham, I took a detour to New Orleans. There, I picked up my two oldest children, Chris and Kathleen, and we traveled together to my sister Judy's house in Savannah for the holiday. At its core, life is about family, and there is nothing better than being surrounded by loved ones on Thanksgiving.

Judy prepared a feast with all the traditional dishes and sides, including turkey, stuffing, mashed potatoes, and pecan pie. I did my best to soak in the moment. The warmth of family time, the laughter, and the glow of love around the table were beautiful.

After the long holiday weekend, I drove back to New Orleans, dropped my children off, hugged them tightly, said goodbye, and then headed for Tampa on Interstate 10. It was the same highway Phil and I had traveled twenty years earlier when we spent the summer at his dad's farm.

As I held the steering wheel of my Acura, I drove along, my mind wandering through memories. That summer with Phil profoundly shaped my life, boosting my confidence, giving me purpose, and inspiring dreams I still chased twenty years later. Once again, I was determined to succeed, to earn enough to finally pursue my dream of becoming a polo player.

As I passed the mile markers on I-10, I decided that this stretch of pavement was my road of dreams. And I wondered: would those dreams ever come true?

As I drove through the night toward Tampa, I took the opportunity to reflect on my many adventures: impulsively moving to Italy, motorcycling across North Africa, sleeping under the stars on the Hill of the Muses opposite the Acropolis, celebrating the spring equinox in the caves of Matala, and enjoying lunch with Peggy Guggenheim at her palazzo in Venice, among others. Despite all I had seen and done, I still felt as if I were just at the beginning of the incredible journey that is my life.

I could not foresee what would unfold or how my future in Tampa would change me, but I had a strong sense that it would. Never in my wildest dreams did I imagine it would completely transform my life and touch tens of thousands of others. That is one of life's greatest wonders: you never know when something good might happen, especially if you work your tail off.

In our first formal meeting, my new partners, Chris Sullivan and Bob Basham, explained that they wanted to emulate the model Rich Melman established with Lettuce Entertain You, a highly successful restaurant group founded in Chicago in 1971. Melman's philosophy centered on the power of partnership: sharing responsibilities and ideas, growing and developing together, and fostering a "culture of caring" at every Lettuce Entertain You location.

By the mid-1980s, Lettuce Entertain You operated more than 130 restaurants across a dozen states, many in the Chicago metro area. The restaurants were distinctive, varied in price, theme, and cuisine, yet they reliably offered good value. Each one reflected Melman's guiding principle: he was not focused on being the biggest, most successful, or most famous restaurateur. Instead, he highly valued the people who worked for him and felt a strong responsibility to help his employees succeed.

Following that approach, Chris and Bob aimed to create a diverse array of restaurants in Tampa Bay and its surroundings. Their plan was to open multiple steakhouses, develop a new restaurant concept, and eventually explore a third, innovative direction.

With our initial plan set, Chris and Bob established Multi-Venture Parties to leverage Tampa's booming growth and reduce our individual burdens. We all understood that managing a national restaurant chain was typically difficult, tiring, and demanding. Senior management often flew on jets, met with analysts, collaborated with joint-venture partners, and endured long days and nights on the road, away from family and friends. That lifestyle was unappealing to all of us.

All three of us had young children, and we deeply wanted to stay close to home and be involved in their upbringing. I cannot emphasize enough how important this was to us.

By focusing on the Tampa market, we believed we would be rooted in the area, or so we thought at the time, and able to stay close to our families.

Our initial plan was simple: build four or five steakhouses in Tampa. After they became profitable and operational, we planned to move on to a second venture. Still, we did not spend much time discussing what the next idea might be, because our priority was to stay fully focused on Job Number One: perfecting our steakhouse concept from the beginning.

We knew our primary responsibility was to keep our eyes fixed on this goal. We had to stay present and avoid dreaming about distant horizons.

Choosing a name was one of our first and most crucial tasks. A strong name is vital across many business sectors, especially in restaurants. Brands like Cracker Barrel, The Cheesecake Factory, and Hooters evoke immediate, memorable impressions. Customers know what to expect when visiting these spots. This familiarity fosters long-term success, provided the restaurants uphold quality.

The market we aimed for, a quality steakhouse situated between a high-end chophouse and a budget steakhouse, had never been explored before. Picking the right name was an essential step.

One evening, a group of us went to the Brown Derby, a steakhouse in Madeira Beach built to resemble a Spanish galleon on the Intracoastal waterway. In the bar where we sat, a mirror hung over our long table. One of the women in our group pulled lipstick from her purse and began writing possible names on the mirror. Yes, this was how sophisticated we were in the beginning, holding court in a bar inside a ship, using a mirror as our whiteboard and lipstick as our marker.

Sipping cocktails, we began brainstorming names. From the start, we all agreed that no suggestion was too silly. We just tossed as many names as possible onto the wall, almost literally, to see if one would stick.

Many of the candidates had a Western twang and theme, but that market was already crowded. Everyone liked the name Montana's, but its chances as a leading candidate quickly diminished when we realized that Bonanza was already in business, as were Ponderosa and Golden Corral.

We needed a memorable identity, one that guests would recognize instantly and remember long after they left the restaurant.

Someone at the table mentioned the 1986 film Crocodile Dundee, which was a major box-office success in the United States, earning hundreds of millions of dollars.

As we discussed further, we agreed that Americans really loved everything Australian, from the Bee Gees to Olivia Newton-John to the Australian people themselves, whom most Americans saw as fun-loving, outgoing, friendly, adventurous, and casual. These were precisely the adjectives that described the vibe we aimed to create. Millions of Americans admired our Australian allies, but no one had capitalized on this connection.

None of us had ever visited Australia, but our interest in an Aussie-themed restaurant grew as we discussed it. Then, someone pointed out that Steak and Ale was an English-themed steakhouse with faux Tudor architecture. Given that England sent its outlaws to Australia, it seemed fitting to create a more daring concept than the place where we had begun our careers, using Steak and Ale as our training ground.

Someone asked, "What is the Wild West of Australia?"

"The Outback!" several of us said in unison.

"Then we should call it Outback Steakhouse," someone proposed.

The motion received unanimous approval. In that moment, we finalized our name. We maintained our Western theme, but it now included a distinctive twist that none of us expected to be so successful.

None of us had ever set foot in Australia, but we were determined to get the feel right. We hired as many Australians as we could for the first few restaurants and learned from them. Their mannerisms, the "good day, mate," and the way they carried themselves with a casualness that never felt careless.

Those early hires taught us more than any research trip could have. Years later, we made many trips to Australia, and each one deepened our understanding of the culture. That deeper immersion shaped everything, from our casual service style to the decision to list each restaurant's leader not as a general manager but as a proprietor, a term borrowed directly from the pubs and bars of Australia.

Now it was time to develop a detailed, step-by-step plan for success. From the start, I was the third wheel, or, more precisely, the fourth wheel. Chris and Bob had both worked with Trudy Cooper, who would play a vital role in launching Outback while raising her family.

Trudy's remarkable insight was rooted in her experience as a schoolteacher. She spent years learning to engage with people not at eye level, whether they were sitting at a classroom desk or a restaurant table. Her straightforward yet impactful solution for our servers was to advise them to lean over when speaking with customers. Some even went further, sitting next to guests in the booths while taking their orders.

There were a few times when customers complained about this practice, preferring that servers maintain a greater distance. We could have banned it outright, but thanks to Trudy's insistence, we allowed our servers to be themselves and trusted their judgment to act naturally and comfortably. Today, leaning over to speak with patrons remains a common practice among Outback servers, contributing to the friendly, approachable environment we envisioned from the very beginning.

Although Chris and I had known each other for fifteen years, our only professional interaction had been as general manager and trainee.

In contrast, Chris, Bob, and Trudy had already joined forces to build a thriving chain of Chili's franchises in Florida, which they eventually sold to Norman Brinker and Brinker International. They knew how to launch restaurants successfully, a key reason I felt confident in our group.

For them, Multi-Venture Partners was their second act.

Chris was the visionary who motivated all of us and himself to aim higher, do better, and move faster. Bob was the calming voice, the steady hand who ensured we stayed on schedule, followed the correct order, and paid attention to every detail, no matter how small. And Trudy was the creator of our culture, both in our restaurants and within our corporate team. Who built our "No Rules, Just Right" attitude that influenced everything we did? That was all Trudy.

The idea behind our motto was simple yet powerful: we would break the rules and do whatever it took to deliver the perfect dining experience every time, for every customer. It became the core of our culture and the heartbeat of Outback.

My role was in the flavor world. I knew that if I could create an unforgettable menu, one full of flavors unlike any other, we would be set up for success. One of my first requests of Bob and Chris was that they join me in New Orleans for a food sampling tour. They needed to experience firsthand the flavors I wanted to bring to Outback Steakhouse.

Upon arriving in the Big Easy, I contacted Warren Leruth to reserve his top table. He agreed, and as expected, Warren's culinary expertise impressed my new partners. While the cuisine and prices at LeRuth's were quite different from Outback's, Warren's commitment to quality was evident in every aspect.

One of the first things Warren did after Chris, Bob, and I sat down for dinner was approach our table with a large wooden-handled steak knife, which he handed to Bob.

"If you're going to do a steakhouse, you've got to use a great steak knife," Warren said.

Bob was impressed by Warren's honesty and advice. Here was a man he did not know personally, truly attempting to help us. The same steak knife would later be the one we used at Outback.

After the meal, Bob and Chris understood why I had wanted to hire Warren as a consulting chef for Outback. They shared my admiration for him, just as I had for years. Warren accepted to join our team in that role, a position he would maintain permanently.

One of Warren's earliest contributions was helping me craft our menu. His attention to detail extended far beyond ingredient measurements; he even specified the required BTUs (British Thermal

Units) for each dish. I had never encountered such a deep commitment to quality. Warren integrated that dedication into the very essence of Outback, embedding it in every Outbacker for years. Warren was a savant, focused on getting everything exactly right, down to the last detail.

In addition to Warren, George Rhode was instrumental in shaping the Outback menu.

George served as the apprentice chef at Commander's Palace under the renowned Cajun chef Paul Prudhomme, who created blackened redfish. He was part of the team that prepared the dish for President Reagan's economic summit in Williamsburg. As Paul's sous chef, he was considered a prodigy. Every dish he crafted was flawless and required no second attempt. He consistently achieved perfect flavor on his first attempt, demonstrating pure genius.

At the time, George was the corporate chef at Copeland's and could not work for us directly under contract. But he always answered my phone calls. We stopped by his restaurant on an R&D trip, and in one day, he rolled out eight dishes that are still on the menu today, thirty-five years later, with recipes that have never changed.

Since George could not accept payment from us due to his contract, I told him that once it expired, I would find a way to take care of him. And so I did.

After five years, I delivered on my promise. I knew George lived in Folsom, Louisiana, in the countryside with a large backyard. So I built him a two-story test kitchen: the upper level served as a library filled with his favorite books and recipes, while the lower level housed a modern, fully equipped kitchen with the latest appliances.

I kept my word, and he kept his.

George later became the corporate chef at Outback, overseeing new menu items for thirty years. He was my culinary partner, and together we created magic over and over.

But that partnership was still years away; we first had to build a restaurant.

In Tampa, Bob warmly welcomed me. I initially stayed in a budget hotel because I had limited time and funds to find better housing. However, Bob did something unforgettable: he invited me to stay at his home for the first six weeks. This gesture showed me that Bob is not only a partner but also a true friend.

But the best part was that Bob's home kitchen turned into my test kitchen, even though I almost burned down his house.

Outback was a startup with limited resources, so we had no choice but to use Bob's residential Jenn-Air stove as our test kitchen, a far cry from the commercial ventilation system designed to handle intense heat and heavy smoke.

One afternoon, I set up in Bob's kitchen to capture the bold flavors of blackened redfish à la Paul Prudhomme. The technique required an extremely hot cast-iron skillet. When I laid the seasoned fish in the pan, it hissed and sputtered, sending a fragrant cloud of smoke that immediately overwhelmed the stove's small downdraft vent. The heat intensified, and the smoke thickened until, suddenly, flames leapt from the pan, climbing higher and higher, eventually licking the curtains at the kitchen window.

Panicked and fearing the worst, I turned off the burner and quickly poured water on the flames. For a few seconds, I believed the house was doomed and that I might be removed as a partner. After all, who would want to stay with someone who burned down their house? Fortunately, we extinguished the flames and averted disaster.

Once we were sure the house was not going to go up in flames, we uncorked a bottle of wine, ate some delicious redfish, which I managed not to ruin amid the chaos, and shared a good laugh. Still, I could not help but think: if that fire had engulfed the house, the idea of Outback might have burned down before we ever opened our first restaurant.

Another note about Bob's house: Years after selling it, he noticed the property was relisted. Curious, he checked the online listing. To his surprise and delight, the agent mentioned that 2912 Villa Rosa was the birthplace of Outback Steakhouse. The real estate agent got it exactly right.

When Bob told me the story, one thing came to mind: the close call with the fire that nearly destroyed the building and possibly Outback Steakhouse.

But as remarkable as it was that Outback Steakhouse almost ended before it began, something even more legendary was still to come. Little did anyone know that the next chapter would introduce a culinary creation that would take the world by storm and forever change the Outback story.

Thirteen

The Bloomin' Onion

Chris Sullivan was completely enraptured by the Onion Mum I served at Copeland's. Its taste, texture, and irresistible nature won him over, turning him into a loyal enthusiast. That is the power of great food: it leaves you craving more, lingers in your mind after the last bite, and even sparks daydreams. Reflecting the restaurant's style and character, Chris believed the deep-fried onion I crafted would become a bestseller and a staple on our growing menu.

The Bloomin' Onion was, after all, an inexpensive appetizer made from a single vegetable, costing fifty cents per pound and suitable for sharing among two, three, or even four people. When we launched Outback, we planned to charge less than four dollars for the appetizer.

Chris named it. He had a gift for applying the Australian theme to everything on our menu, whether it was the Crocodile Dundee Strip Steak, the Alice Springs Chicken, or the Outback Special. When he saw the onion, he knew exactly what to call it.

Down in Australia, "bloomin'" is how they add weight to a word. It also describes exactly what happens when that onion hits the fryer: it blooms. The petals open, and the whole thing becomes something bigger than it was. That was Chris. He could look at a thing, find the one word that held it all together, and make you remember it forever. The Bloomin' Onion was born. Today, our parent company is called Bloomin' Brands in honor of our Bloomin' Onion.

The real value of this tasty appetizer was evident when paired with a drink. Not offering a Foster's or a Wallaby Darned meant missing out on extra revenue and enhancing the guest experience. These add-ons could double the bill before the main courses, boosting profits. Our pricing strategy, whether for prime rib or a large New Zealand rack of lamb, was deliberately crafted to maximize opportunities while still ensuring customer satisfaction, with or without the extras.

From the first bite of the onion appetizer, Chris saw its potential for profit. He encouraged us to upsell at every turn, and his keen eye set the standard. I eagerly followed his lead.

My journey to turn a billion-dollar idea into our upcoming restaurant's reality started with a single overwhelming emotion: fear. I did not anticipate how challenging it would be to develop what ultimately became the Bloomin' Onion. Looking back, I see this was partly my own fault; I had overlooked one of Bud Heatley's key lessons from years ago—the significance of time.

How long did it take Swiss engineer George de Mestral to develop Velcro? At least a decade. How many steps were needed to create a hook-and-loop fastener that mimicked how a burr stuck to a dog's coat? The loop part was simple. But the hook? That required de Mestral years to refine, tweak, and finally perfect. In fact, it was not until after World War II ended and DuPont's nylon became widely available that de Mestral finished the hook.

Developing the Bloomin' Onion took years of work, especially since I had already been experimenting with it for about two years in the test kitchen at Copeland's. The first challenge was finding the perfect onion. After selecting it, I prepared it to perfection. The final touch was the dipping sauce, which had to be flawless; otherwise, the appetizer would lack the impact I desired.

Finally, perhaps the most overlooked aspect of developing the Bloomin' Onion was the production challenge. Making just a few blooms in a test kitchen was not enough; we needed to figure out how to produce thousands of blooms daily.

Let us start by looking at how these challenges were addressed, beginning with the onion itself. The onions used in our commercial kitchens were quite different from those typically found in local grocery store produce sections.

Early in the 20th century, onions were bred primarily to fit in a woman's hand. Because women handled most household shopping and cooking, onions were cultivated to this size. Store-bought onions typically weigh between half a pound and three-quarters of a pound. Seeing one close to a full pound is almost as rare as finding a four-leaf clover. In short, onions of that size are seldom shipped to stores and rarely reach consumers.

But I needed something different.

I wanted a large onion that could comfortably serve up to four people. It needed to have a single heart, the bulb at its very center. Typically, onions around 3 inches in diameter develop a second heart. Larger onions require two hearts to grow properly, which creates a challenge during preparation. Our straightforward rule was: one heart is good, two hearts are not.

Early on, we found that making the Bloomin' Onion required onions with a single heart, which ensured customers got more onion. This detail reflects Outback's core philosophy of always putting the customer first, a principle that was key to our overall success.

After outlining the essential criteria for a successful appetizer, I began searching for America's top onion expert to consult. I found him at Texas A&M in College Station.

Dr. Leonard Pike, who passed away in 2019, was a distinguished research scientist who dedicated much of his career to Texas A&M AgriLife as a horticulture professor and vegetable breeder. His specialties included onions and carrots, and he was so skilled that he founded Texas A&M's Vegetable and Fruit Improvement Center. To this day, farmers in South Texas revere Leonard Pike as the creator of the Texas 1015 Supersweet, a delicious yellow onion that grows well in Texas's Rio Grande Valley, the same land where I once rode horses with Phil Heatley in my early youth.

Few people on the planet could discuss onions with the same enthusiasm, insight, and knowledge as Dr. Pike. The more I explained the concept of the Bloomin' Onion, the more questions he asked. What was the flavor profile? What was the perfect portion size? Would Outback serve the Blooms year-round or seasonally?

When I explained that we had cored the onion so it would have only one heart, he immediately understood what I was trying to do. The excitement in his voice, first over the phone and then in person, made it clear to me that I had found the right person to seek help and guidance.

After I described the many qualities I was looking for in the Bloom, Dr. Pike almost immediately pinpointed the onion I needed: a particular seed of the Spanish Colossal, a sweet yellow onion weighing 1.25 pounds. That is at least half a pound more than a typical store-bought onion. Once a Spanish Colossal is peeled and prepared, it weighs about one pound, a perfect sharing size.

The Spanish Colossal onion offered another advantage: its sweetness. With lower sulfur levels, it lacked the sharp bite typical of white onions. Another benefit was its single heart, which allowed it to grow large without producing a second heart. However, it had high water content, which reduced its shelf life and necessitated securing a reliable year-round supply. Despite this drawback, I was determined to make it work because the benefits clearly outweighed the disadvantages.

The first step was complete: we had chosen the Spanish Colossal onion for the Bloom. But now new problems have arisen, especially the need for a specialized grower for this unique onion. Despite its size, the Spanish Colossal was fragile, almost delicate, complex, and hard to grow.

Dr. Pike surprised me by explaining that the best place to grow a Spanish Colossal onion is in the Snake River Valley of Idaho and Eastern Oregon. This large, fertile area produces a quarter of America's onions. It is also known for Idaho Russet potatoes, which supply major brands such as McDonald's and Lay's. Each year, billions of French fries and potato chips are made from crops grown here. Because of its strong agricultural reputation, Outback's Bloomin' Onion should originate from such a respected food region.

As Outback expanded and opened new locations, we increasingly relied on the Kingston family in Idaho as a primary supplier of Spanish Colossal onions. The Kingstons oversaw not only the cultivation of these onions but also their storage, along with many other onion varieties, baking and frying potatoes, and various vegetables, all stored in large warehouses maintained at low temperatures with reduced oxygen levels to preserve freshness. These large facilities, resembling airplane hangars, enabled us to ship Spanish Colossals directly from the farm across the country and, most importantly, offer our Bloomin' Onions year-round.

After several discussions with Dr. Pike, it became clear that the Spanish Colossal was the ideal onion for the Bloom. With that decision made, I moved on to the next step, my specialty: crafting the flavor profiles of the deep-fried onion and the dipping sauce.

My goal was straightforward yet challenging: to develop that signature comeback flavor in both the bloom and the sauce. Do you remember that term? It is the one I learned in New Orleans, and to me, it is what separates success from failure in the restaurant business. If you craft a memorable dining experience with exceptional flavor, guests will keep coming back and bring friends to share the same great food again and again.

Bottom line: if you have a comeback flavor, you have a winning restaurant.

This idea reflects a mantra that Norman Brinker, who mentored me, Steve, and Chris during our time at Steak and Ale, often reiterated. Norman's most cherished saying was: "There's only one sacred thing in the restaurant business, and that is the customer's intent to return."

Norman believed that perfecting every detail, from ambiance and staff interactions to food consistency, was crucial for customer retention. Food was central to Norman's philosophy and aligned with my expertise. As a flavorist, I strived to craft flavors so refined that ordinary dishes turned extraordinary, making every guest's visit unforgettable.

Realizing I could not do this alone, I asked Warren Leruth to join me on this critical project, which could be either our path to wealth or a path that would lead to shrinking bank accounts. I wanted to include George Rhode IV as well, but he was still employed at Copeland's under a non-compete agreement. So, it was just Warren and me, working in Bob's kitchen, the same one I almost set on fire, to discover the perfect flavors that would define not only the Bloomin' Onion but all of Outback's signature dishes.

Crafting the ideal seasoning combination for both the batter and the dipping sauce was challenging. It involved hundreds of tweaks, including preparing, tasting, noting, and repeating.

We often had to scrap entire batches and start over from scratch. It took numerous trials before we reached the perfect flavor profiles for the Bloomin' Onion, which used seventeen spices in the batter and thirty-seven in the sauce. To this day, those spice blends remain unchanged and unmatched. This special spice mix is what gives Outback food its unique and recognizable taste.

Warren Leruth and I became food chemists around the same time. Warren began as a baker, precisely measuring each ingredient, a trait common among bakers. I brought four years of experience from working with Al Copeland, where chains like Popeye's depended on exact timing for everything. Together, we turned every step of making the Bloomin' Onion into a systematic process: Warren handled

The Bloomin' Onion

the details, while I ensured the workflow was efficient and seamless.

Even now, I can distinguish whether a Bloom was cooked at 345 or 355 degrees. In cooking, seemingly minor details are crucial, especially with the Bloom, where precise frying temperature is essential. I can tell when a Bloomin' Onion is not perfectly cooked because if it does not fry in 350-degree oil for two and a half minutes per side, the result will be off. Fry for less time, and it is undercooked; fry longer, and it tastes burnt.

Cooking with unwavering precision and a profound respect for flavor became my guiding principle.

However, making the Bloomin' Onion soon proved to be a challenge beyond my skill set. Dr. Leonard Pike suggested using a 1.25-pound Spanish Colossal onion, which was perfect.

The real challenge, though, was on our end: we still had to make numerous manual cuts and remove the onion core by hand. As de-

With Steve Harvey and a Bloomin' Onion.

mand grew, production became slow and labor-intensive, and every cut had to be perfectly consistent from onion to onion.

Improving our cutting technique was essential; without it, high labor costs could have jeopardized the company's very existence. That is how I met Gloria.

For the first few years after we opened in 1988, every Bloomin' Onion was sliced by hand before being battered and fried. It was slow, labor-intensive work. In 1991, I finally found a manufacturer who could build a slicing machine exclusively for Outback Steakhouse.

As an altar boy at Saint Anthony's Catholic Church in Fort Lauderdale, I learned the Latin phrase "Gloria in excelsis deo," which means "Glory to God in the highest." When I first saw what this machine could do, transforming a Spanish Colossal into a beautiful bloom with over two hundred petals, that phrase came to mind. I named her Gloria.

Although expensive, I recognized her importance to our success. Today, many versions are available online, but I was the first to order one. Despite the cost, I knew the investment would pay off.

How vital is Gloria's role? Let me highlight her contributions. At the time of this writing, one out of every four appetizers at Outback Steakhouse is a Bloomin' Onion. Many have tried to replicate my idea, including Chili's with the Awesome Blossom, Lone Star Steakhouse with the Texas Rose, and Texas Roadhouse with the Cactus Blossom. However, none have surpassed the Bloomin' Onion's enduring popularity. The original recipe remains unchanged.

The numbers are astonishing: over 17 million Bloomin' Onions are sold annually. More impressively, sales have surpassed $1 billion, making it the best-selling appetizer ever.

We first announced that milestone on the Steve Harvey Show in Chicago. Steve's eyes went wide when I told him the number. A billion dollars from a single appetizer. Even on national television, despite his extensive experience, he was amazed. It showed the world the scope of what we had built, an onion served in twenty-seven countries, from Japan to South Korea to Brazil, that had crossed a threshold no appetizer in casual dining had ever reached.

It is hard for me to believe, but my Velcro became a billion-dollar business.

It was built around a single appetizer.

Fourteen

The Launch of Outback

The Bloomin' Onion was just one of my culinary creations at Outback. I used the Bloomin' Onion's seasonings and spices to make our so-called "puddle of richness," a dark brown noisette butter we seared into all our steaks. Even before opening our first restaurant, we thought our most popular steak would be the Outback Special, a 12-ounce sirloin served with steamed vegetables and a salad for $9.95. We believed that this combination of value and flavor would set us on the road to success.

Our first Outback was at 3403 Henderson Boulevard, though it was far from an ideal location. The bar sat in an old, worn-down strip mall, and when we signed the lease, the space was in rough shape: it reeked of alcohol and needed a thorough cleaning. With limited funds, we kept expenses to a minimum by choosing the cheapest flooring we could find, reclaimed from an old basketball court.

We gathered most of our décor from antique shops. Our walls featured bullhorns, sheep shears, boomerangs, kangaroo posters, shark jaws, stuffed koalas, and surfboards. Plus, a partner's friend donated an old pair of rugby shoes, which we proudly hung on the wall.

We decided not to visit Australia before our grand opening to avoid the temptation to add authentic Australian dishes that might not appeal to American tastes.

Instead, we developed an all-American menu while fostering an atmosphere that pays tribute to Australia's vibrant spirit, culture, and warmth, ranging from its adventurous nature to its relaxed hospitality. On the night before opening, the four of us founders arrived with a six-pack of beer and decorated the space ourselves.

Opening Night on March 15, 1988, was filled with anticipation. We were excited as we prepared for our first guests, but when we opened the doors, no one came in. The restaurant was so quiet I

The original founders of Outback Steakhouse. Tim Gannon, Bob Basham, Trudy Cooper, Chris Sullivan

could hear the ice machine humming in the kitchen.

Panicked, we called friends and asked them to bring more people. Despite our efforts, that first night was very slow, and I worried we might fail. Unlike most restaurants that thrive on opening-night energy, ours had only a few college students drinking loudly at the bar.

The problem was that only our friends knew about Outback. I focused primarily on developing the Bloomin' Onion and the menu, while others handled specific tasks to prepare the restaurant. As a result, our marketing and promotion efforts were ineffective. In the early weeks, we attracted very few customers, so we asked employees to park directly in front of the restaurant to create the impression of a busy establishment.

After seeing empty tables every night for about a month, I fell into a depression, convinced we would fail and that financial ruin was imminent. One evening, around 10:30 p.m., I left the restaurant alone and headed to a small pizza place with a tiny bar around the corner on Mac Dill Avenue. The fluorescent light buzzed overhead, and a television no one was watching played quietly in the corner.

My plan was simple: order a beer and quietly brood.

As I sat on a stool, pondering my difficult financial situation, I overheard a couple at the bar. To my surprise, they were talking about the Bloomin' Onion — my onion!

"Oh my God, it's the most incredible thing I have ever had," the man said to his companion. "I can't wait to tell more people about it."

I smiled brighter than ever, realizing in that moment that we would succeed!

The following day at the restaurant, Chris Sullivan approached me with a serious expression. He placed his arm on my shoulder and confessed that he was deeply concerned we might have to close permanently if conditions did not improve quickly. While holding a menu, he asked, "Did you get this food right?" It was clear he was blaming our sluggish start on the menu we provided.

That was my moment. For years, I had deferred to others, doubted myself, and wondered whether I belonged. But not this time. I looked Chris in the eye and said, "The only thing we got right was the food."

I did not back down. "We are on a side street and have not done any marketing. People do not know who we are or where we are. We are in an area where other restaurants and bars have already closed. I know you are used to working with chain restaurants that have a name and a brand, like Chili's and Bennigan's, but that is not us. We are a non-branded restaurant, and none of us has ever opened one of these before. The location is wrong. The marketing is wrong. The name is unrecognizable. Australian Steakhouse makes no sense to people. So we have problems. But the food? The food is right."

Chris listened. He got it. He understood. "Good," he said. "I am glad I do not have to worry about the food. Let us start marketing the place."

That is precisely what we did.

We started our days at six in the morning, visiting radio stations, cooking meals for on-air personalities in the hallways, and going live to explain why Outback stood out from other American steakhouses. After tasting our food, the DJs would rave for days, praising its flavor and sending their listeners our way. Nearly every time, they singled out the Bloomin' Onion, calling it unlike anything they had ever tasted and the best appetizer they had ever had.

Outback's founders (left to right): Tim Gannon, Bob Basham and Chris Sullivan.

We did not know if it would work. The first weekend after the radio spots aired, there was a brief wait at the door for the first time. I stood by the host stand, watching people walk in, hardly believing it. The next week, the wait was longer. The week after that, longer still. Within a month, the line stretched out the door and into the parking lot. Strangers were asking strangers what was good, and every single one of them ordered the Bloomin' Onion.

One evening, after experiencing a crowded restaurant, Chris came up to me and said, "You know what? You did get the food right. You got it REALLY right."

To this day, in over 1,400 Outbacks across 28 countries, where 17 languages are spoken, the menu remains essentially the same as the one we used at that first Outback in South Tampa. Chris has repeatedly told me how much he appreciates my dedication to crafting our dishes. The proof is in the success: I got the food right.

One of the best compliments I ever received about Outback's menu came from my partner, Bob Basham. "Tim brought the flavors to the table, and that's what made Outback stand out," Bob said. "He understood flavors because he had been involved in restaurants in New Orleans, where seasonings make the food craveable. If we'd launched the concept based on Chris's experience or my experience, it would have been a combination of Steak and Ale and Bennigan's. And we would not have had a thousand restaurants around the world."

Celebrities quickly started visiting our first Outback. Willie Nelson dropped by one evening, and General Norman Schwarzkopf came with friends on another night. On the night before Super Bowl XXV in Tampa, where Whitney Houston performed her iconic national anthem, Giants' Ottis Anderson visited and ordered two steaks. He was named MVP the next day after rushing for 102 yards and scoring two touchdowns in a 20–19 win.

Within just a few months of launching our promotional and advertising campaign, we had queuing lines of people eager to enter Outback. To leverage this success, we promptly opened a second location in North Tampa on June 1, 1988, and then another in Sarasota on September 15.

One evening at the Sarasota Outback, a renowned food critic from the St. Petersburg Times walked in. Famous for being nearly impossible to impress, he had built his reputation on his exacting standards. He took a seat alone, notepad in hand, and ordered several dishes. I watched from a distance, reluctant to interrupt. Only

The original Outback Steakhouse.

The original Outback Steakhouse entrance.

as he rose to leave did I finally approach him.

"This is a restaurant run by three food-chain guys," he told me. "It looks like your average chain restaurant, with the wood floor, booths, and the central bar. But my goodness: once you take that first bite of food, it's no longer a chain restaurant. The food is magical."

The following day, we received our most favorable early review yet, published in the St. Petersburg Times. The article boosted awareness of Outback and promoted our culinary message to a broad audience. Soon after, critics from across the state and region began visiting our three Outback locations and writing positive reviews. It was as if a spark had been ignited, and the fire of success was just beginning to grow.

Although our three restaurants were busy, I faced financial challenges. We reinvested almost all profits in the business to expand rapidly. To cover living expenses, I drew a $50,000 salary. However, with two young children and substantial debt from the World's Fair disaster and from the I.R.S., my discretionary income was limited. Essentially, I was still broke.

Early in my time at Outback, my children were counting down the days to Christmas, and I was counting the dollars I did not have.

Kathleen wanted dolls and a small pony toy. Chris wanted toy race cars. I could not afford any of it, and I felt like a complete failure. What kind of father cannot give his children gifts from Santa? It was one of the lowest moments of my life.

Then a friend stepped in. She was a single mom who worked as a secretary for my landlord. When she learned I did not have a Christmas tree, she immediately understood my situation. She went out and bought a tree, decorated it, and set it up in my apartment. She also went shopping for my children, making sure she bought exactly what they had asked for in their letters to Santa. The tree, the decorations, and a couple of presents added up to less than a hundred dollars. It was a hundred dollars I did not have.

On Christmas morning, I watched my children eagerly open their presents, their smiles so bright they lit the room. I have never forgotten what she did for my family.

Even though I was embarrassed by my lack of funds, I never voiced my concerns to my partners about my modest income. I was confident things would improve, and we would have more than enough money for everyone.

My partners were honest, intelligent, and had a great sense of humor. As a single dad, I was always fighting a losing battle to keep my car clean; my children constantly turned the back seat into chaos. No matter how often I cleaned it, the vehicle would be messy again the moment they got in, as if the mess appeared instantly. My Acura's messiness quickly became a running joke among my partners.

I eventually bought a car from Bob, using a 12 percent loan he arranged for me. Before handing me the keys, he grinned mischievously and said, "Selling my car to you is like taking my dog to the pound." We both laughed.

Years later, after Outback's success and once I finally had the funds to settle the loan, I drove to his house with the check. Bob was so tight with money that he was annoyed when I arrived at noon, because it meant he could not collect a full day's interest. Looking back, I have to admit I may have timed it that way on purpose.

In those early days with just three restaurants, Chris, Bob, and I worked tirelessly. Each night, one of us would visit every location to ensure smooth operations, greet customers, and handle staff issues. We often worked long, late hours, determined to be on-site and ensure everything was as close to perfect as possible.

I often lingered in the kitchen, paying close attention to how each item was prepared. Seeing many Bloomin' Onions on the tables and the satisfaction on customers' faces as they enjoyed my appetizer was always rewarding. These moments reminded me why all the sacrifices were worth it.

Before Outback, I served thousands of excellent meals yet never achieved true financial success. That changed when I partnered with Chris, Bob, and Trudy, and the money finally started pouring in. Why? It was not because I was working harder than I had at the World's Fair. It was because I had found the right partners whose strengths complemented mine, and that made all the difference.

One example of their collective ingenuity was the managing partner model. Each Outback Steakhouse had a managing partner, and his or her name was engraved right on the front door. Traditionally, in the restaurant industry, the top person is called a general manager. But as a nod to our Aussie theme, we listed their names as the "Proprietor."

Here is the clever part: for $25,000, the proprietor, the managing partner, got ten percent equity in the restaurant they managed.

Essentially, our steakhouse turned into their steakhouse. We invested in them, and they invested in us. It was a win-win for both parties and played a crucial role in launching the startup.

We no longer considered restaurant operators as employees; instead, we viewed them as partners. And believe me, they proved to be some of the best partners in the industry. Why? Because no other casual dining chain provided seasoned professionals with a deal as attractive as Outback's. This sweat equity allowed Outback to enter a highly competitive industry with experienced restaurateurs on the front lines who required much less supervision.

As we expanded, we noticed a pattern: most managing partners began their journey at Outback as hourly workers. The optional $25,000 investment to become a managing partner helped ensure full financial and personal commitment.

We then gave managing partners considerable independence, including authority over hiring. We stressed that every hiring decision could affect the entire team, because even one problematic employee, such as a poorly performing dishwasher, could disrupt operations for everyone.

Working closely with the people they hired enabled our partners to better understand employees' concerns and aspirations. For instance, they would not expect someone balancing college studies to cover four or more shifts in a single week. We never wanted our restaurants to become revolving doors for employees, since returning customers like seeing a familiar face.

How do you retain talented employees? At Steak and Ale, I observed that issues such as a cramped kitchen or dull knives could deter skilled staff. As a result, Bob Basham was committed to making all our kitchens at least 2,500 square feet and ensuring good airflow, even if it increased costs.

The kitchens occupied half of the typical Outback restaurant's layout, a space that other chains usually reserved for revenue-generating tables. However, because our goal was to offer a broader menu than most casual restaurants in the 1980s, Bob and Chris recognized the importance of giving the cooks and prep staff ample room to manage it effectively.

Unlike most restaurants, our server management strategy truly sets us apart. At Outback, we capped each server to three tables, compared to the industry norm of five or six.

Positioned between Morton's and Ponderosa, Outback attracted an eclectic mix of guests, from sports fans catching a game to people celebrating major life milestones. By limiting servers to just three tables, we delivered attentive, personalized service that elevated the dining experience and built lasting customer loyalty.

According to Bob and Chris's restaurant Bible, the customer should dictate the pace of the meal, not the server or kitchen staff. To achieve this, our servers needed to read the mood and expectations of each table every night. The kitchen had to be staffed and equipped to turn around orders swiftly, and the recipes needed to be simple and straightforward. If servers were responsible for too many tables, they could not accurately judge how quickly each customer wanted their food.

> *"He'll give you the shirt off his back…it would be too big for me, but he will give you the shirt off his back. He is someone who is just willing to share and has done a lot of good for a lot of people."*
>
> ᐳ *Bob Basham*

Bob Basham: 'He'll give you the shirt off his back.'

One of the most significant innovations by Bob, Chris, and Trudy was choosing not to serve lunch. They made this choice for several reasons.

First, they wanted to avoid overburdening their servers, who would otherwise have to cover both lunch and dinner shifts. Second, if they offered lunch, the restaurant manager could work up to eighty hours a week. Finally, preparing food early for lunch risked a loss of quality by dinnertime, which could undermine the overall dining experience.

Since most Outback locations are in suburban areas, we realized we would miss the profitable downtown business lunch crowd, a significant source of lunchtime revenue and high-margin drink sales. As a result, serving lunch was not a practical option for us.

Bob, Chris, and Trudy emphasized the importance of connecting our managing partners to Outback's history. From the beginning, we established a tradition called "The Walkabout," held several times a year. Each manager was invited to Tampa for an office tour and a meeting with the four founders, culminating in dinner at one of the founders' homes. This experience forged a unique bond between Outback's leadership and its founders, cultivating a culture of closeness and trust seldom seen in the restaurant industry.

Initially, our business strategy focused on strengthening our core markets, namely Tampa and Sarasota. We then planned to expand into Southern and Western Florida by opening new restaurants in Fort Lauderdale, Miami, Hollywood, and elsewhere. As our success and profits grew, we adopted a bolder approach. In one year, we opened 160 Outback restaurants, and our business flourished.

I often smile when I think about our original "grand plan" to open five steakhouses in the Tampa Bay area. After those were up and running, Multi-Venture Partners intended to launch a second concept, then a third. Fate, however, had other ideas.

The long lines and strong per-unit sales made it clear to Bob, Chris, and Trudy that Outback, and only Outback, should be our primary focus. Those first five restaurants were just the beginning. In the end, the appeal of my flavors, supported by my partners' and our team's exceptional management, helped Outback grow to more than 1,400 locations in 28 countries.

> *"Without Tim's diligence in making sure that Bloomin' Onion' became successful, I doubt Outback would have become the huge success it became."*
>
> ભ *Chris Sullivan*

Chris Sullivan on the Bloomin' Onion and Outback's success.

But success was never easy. As we grew, demand for high-quality beef intensified, and the beef market proved volatile. One year, the price of our number one product skyrocketed by 35%. Chris Sullivan

*On the cover of F&B magazine,
November 1993.*

*F&B Magazine on the Bloomin'
Onion story, November 1993.*

came to me and said, "We have to fix this meat purchasing problem. If we do not, it will destroy us."

Chris then mentioned an old friend: Billy Rosenthal of Standard Meat Company in Fort Worth, Texas. Standard Meat had been in business since 1935, founded by Billy's grandfather, Ben Rosenthal.

Billy's family had deep roots in the meat industry, and his company had sold steaks to Norman Brinker at Steak and Ale, the very restaurant where Chris and I first crossed paths. Once again, the threads of my life were weaving together in ways I could not have predicted.

There was one problem. Billy had stepped away from Standard Meat and was now in the pizza business, making pepperoni. But Chris believed Billy was the right man, and Chris was rarely wrong about people.

I called Billy and asked if he would help me resolve our purchasing and pricing issues. He agreed. Billy knew the beef business inside and out. He understood what suppliers could do, how to streamline their operations, and how to negotiate prices that would protect us as we scaled. He had so many good ideas that I quickly realized he was not just a consultant. He was the one who would take us through every beef challenge we would face as a national company.

And there were many. Mad Cow Disease made people wary of

red meat. Food safety became an urgent issue across our growing restaurant system. Billy guided us through it all. His expertise and steady hand kept our supply chain intact when lesser companies would have stumbled.

After working together closely, I said, "Billy, you need to be our meat supplier."

He had no meat plant. But Billy knew he could use a friend's factory to get started. More importantly, he understood what Outback was becoming. His own father had helped Steak and Ale grow into a national chain, and Billy wanted to duplicate that path of success with us.

With nothing more than a handshake, Billy invested $35 million to build a meat-processing plant for one customer: Outback Steakhouse. No contract. No lawyers. Just two men who trusted each other and believed in what they were building together.

That handshake launched a partnership that has endured for more than 30 years. Today, Standard Meat Company remains our primary supplier, with annual revenue approaching $1 billion and five processing plants.

Billy's son, Ben Rosenthal, and his daughter, Ashli Rosenthal Blumenfeld, now lead the company as the fourth-generation family owners. In 2024, Ben and Ashli were named Ernst & Young's Entrepreneurs of the Year.

The father-son relationship I see between Billy and Ben mirrors what I see in my own family with Chris, in Chris Sullivan and his son Alex, and in Bob Basham and his sons. Passing something meaningful to the next generation is the most compelling measure of success I know.

When I look back at Standard Meat's journey, which began with a handshake just like mine with Phil and mine with Chris Sullivan, I understand what these handshakes are truly about. They are promises about future behavior. Promises made and kept, written in big, bold letters, are the reason any of us are here. And you should never underestimate the power of a simple handshake.

Partnerships like these carried us through what came next. We faced other persistent hurdles beyond the beef market: gas prices soared, the housing market collapsed, and shortly after, the stock market plummeted. Each challenge pushed us, but we consistently navigated these tough times and emerged stronger. These moments proved that true leadership means confronting difficulties head-on rather than dodging them.

Outback Steakhouse quickly gained success, with revenues, profits, and the number of restaurants rising rapidly.

In November 1994, Inc. Magazine invited us to Palm Springs, where we were proud finalists for Ernst & Young's Entrepreneur of the Year Award. We were surprised not only to be included but also by the formidable competition.

I had wondered whether Outback could win. Although we had built a strong steakhouse, companies like Steve Case's America Online were transforming internet access, and Ted Waitt's Gateway 2000 was booming with an innovative mail-order computer business in Sioux City, Iowa. The innovation on display seemed to outpace our own.

By comparison, we were anything but pioneers at Outback. We were industry veterans who had created a better mousetrap. Not a new one, just a better one. And believe it or not, that is why the judges named us Entrepreneurs of the Year.

The judges told Chris Sullivan that only one of us could be named Entrepreneur of the Year. Chris insisted that the award be shared with his two other partners or not given at all. I thought that would rule us out.

I flew my family in from San Francisco to Palm Springs for the banquet for 5,000 applicants. Chris told me that if we won, he would let me give the acceptance speech since my family was there in person. I worked hard on that speech, hoping to use it.

Then they called the three finalists: AOL, Callaway Golf, and us. When they announced Outback as the winner, I jumped up, speech in hand, a smile on my face. I looked out over the crowd of 5,000 and zeroed in on my mother. I saw the pride in her eyes as my partners and I were named Entrepreneurs of the Year. I, the last of six children, was pulling up the caboose in great style: from scratch to glorious success.

We had both done our job.

Harry Quadracci, president of the national printing company Quad/Graphics, remarked, "Outback shows that no industry is too crowded if you have the right idea and put in the hard work."

"These Outback guys pulled off a beautiful ride in Boston Harbor at low tide," said Judge Jeffry Timmons, a business professor at Babson College. "You could almost say they were going against the tide. Who would recommend that you start a steakhouse in this day and age?"

In retrospect, launching Outback seemed risky, yet we were surprised to receive a prestigious award. The 'No Rules, Just Right' idea, and even the name we devised at a bar, transformed Outback into an iconic American brand within six years. But the biggest day was still ahead of us.

Outback just right for U.S. award

By LISA BACKMAN
Tribune Staff Writer

TAMPA — The founders of Outback Steakhouse, who crystalized the Aussie-themed, casual restaurant chain at a Tampa nightclub in 1987, nabbed the coveted national Entrepreneur of the Year award that will put them on the cover of Inc. magazine.

Chairman Chris Sullivan, President Bob Basham and Senior Vice President Tim Gannon will appear on December's cover to be available soon, cinching Tampa-based Outback's place as the first Florida company to win the 8-year-old prize.

Outback leaders beat out finalists California-based Watson Pharmaceuticals, South Dakota-based mail order computer company Gateway 2000, Virginia-based online computer service America Online and Massachusetts-based family service provider Work/Family Directions.

Judges liked Outback's sizzling, innovative concept that has skyrocketed it to success in the mature, highly competitive restaurant industry.

"These Outback guys pulled off a beautiful ride on a surfboard in Boston Harbor at low tide. You could almost say they were going against the tide," said one judge in an Inc. article describing the judging process.

"Who in their right mind would recommend that you start a steakhouse in this day and age?" he added.

They were honored earlier this week at a banquet in Palm Springs, Calif. Chief sponsors include: Inc., Ernst & Young and Merrill Lynch.

Outback has appealed to diners because it offers the right mix of thick, juicy steaks at relatively low prices in a fun, casual atmosphere.

It took off, growing from two restaurants in 1988 to 210 outlets currently. It also has launched Carrabba's Italian Grill, a casual Italian restaurant that will open its first Tampa store next week.

Revenues are expected to reach $544 million this year, up from $347.5 million last year. They are projected to hit $739 million in 1995 and $956 million in 1996.

Earnings growth is expected to be just as strong, settling in the 30 percent to 35 percent range annually, which is extremely high for a restaurant company, said Harry Venezia, restaurant analyst for Raymond James & Associates Inc. in St. Petersburg.

If its stock hits $33 a share, it will become what's known as a "10 bagger" in the investment community, meaning its stock will have risen in value 10 times from its original offering price of $3.33, adjusted for stock splits, Venezia said.

It closed at $30.25 Wednesday, down 12.5 cents.

The Inc. award simply points out what the investment community has known for two years about Outback: That it's one of the three best-managed casual dining restaurants in the country.

"It's already surpassed Cracker Barrel and it's not far behind Brinker," Venezia said. Brinker owns Chili's, Macaroni Grill and others.

Outback's Basham attributes the company's success to all its partners, franchisees and employees.

"It's a nice recognition of everything all of our people have been able to accomplish in the last six years," Basham said.

Winning the prestigious award wasn't tops on his list in the beginning.

"The original idea was to open four or five restaurants in the Tampa Bay area and play golf," he said with a laugh.

Outback Steak House's brain trust will appear on December's cover of Inc. magazine.

Inc. magazine: Entrepreneurs of the Year.

Fifteen

The Day That Changed My Life – Going Public

After one of the most incredible and satisfying workdays of my career, I stepped out of San Francisco's Mandarin Hotel, still beaming. Chris and Bob had left to catch a flight, so I had the limousine to myself. A broad smile spread across my face as I slipped into the backseat of the limo, the chauffeur waiting patiently. He turned to ask, "Where to?"

"Across the Golden Gate Bridge," I replied, barely containing my joy.

To truly understand the importance of this day, it helps to look back on the journey that brought us here. Years ago, armed with little more than a spark of an idea, determination, and the support of friends like Chris and Bob, we began building Outback Steakhouse from the ground up.

From the very beginning, our goal was to create a restaurant that brings people together. Every challenge and victory became part of our story, showing us that even small moments shape our future.

Over time, our persistence paid off. By June 1991, we had opened forty-nine Outback restaurants across the US and beyond. Those years were marked by challenges, sleepless nights, and bold decisions.

I will never forget the early days when no one came through the doors. As I described, Chris questioned me about the food, but it was the only thing we got right. The location was wrong. The marketing was nonexistent. The name confused people. We had great food, but the dining room was empty.

Chris went to work on the problem. He started marketing on morning radio. We earned a write-up in the St. Petersburg Times, which was the spark. From that moment, it was off to the races.

Those recipes I created then are still the ones used today. They have not changed one bit.

To understand why we chose to take Outback public, we should look back to the late 1980s. Going public means selling shares of your company on the stock market for the first time, an IPO, or Initial Public Offering. It is how a privately held company raises large amounts of money from the public. Strangers invest their money because they believe in your business. In return, they own a piece of it.

Outback was thriving, and demand for new locations was outpacing our ability to fund them. Opening a new restaurant requires significant investment, from building out the space to hiring and training staff to purchasing equipment. Multiply that across dozens of locations, and the numbers add up fast.

Meanwhile, the economy was working against us. Banks were failing because of the Savings and Loan crisis, and investors were still reeling from the 1987 stock market crash. Traditional lending had nearly dried up. Going public was not merely about growth. It was essential to our survival.

We came to realize that Outback was truly unique when a struggling Louisville restaurant owner asked Chris for permission to franchise Outback, and Chris agreed. Despite initial challenges, the small, lightly promoted Louisville location succeeded. This surprising success showed that if a modest operation could flourish, others could as well. That moment made us realize that Outback had the potential to expand nationally.

I had been receiving partnership checks from my 20% equity stake, and for the first time in years, I could breathe. Chris and Bob were so committed to the company's growth that neither took a salary. Their integrity was remarkable.

Then Chris came to me with news. The good news was that we were going public. The bad news was that the partnership checks would stop immediately. I would go back to a $50,000 salary while still carrying $280,000 in debt at 18% interest. Going public meant more years of operating lean, more sacrifice, with no guarantee it would pay off.

I did not hesitate. If Chris and Bob believed this was the right path, I was all in. But the sacrifice was real.

My partners and I agreed to accept modest salaries for three years.

Throughout that period, I continued making payments on my debt, even as the interest kept compounding. Bankruptcy might have seemed like the easiest way out, but I refused to consider it. I had made a promise to Tommy Westervelt at Hibernia Bank, and I intended to keep it.

Beyond that, a personal bankruptcy would have been devastating for any company preparing to go public. Underwriters scrutinize every detail of the management team's financial history. A bankruptcy on my record could have undermined investor confidence and jeopardized everything we had built.

Before a company can go public, its founders have to go on what Wall Street calls a road show. You travel from city to city, sitting across the table from the people who manage billions of dollars, and you convince them that your company is worth investing in. If they believe in you, they buy shares. If they do not, your IPO fails.

Our road show was five relentless days. From eight in the morning until ten at night, Chris, Bob, and I told the Outback story to some of the world's most powerful investors. Fidelity. Goldman Sachs. Peter Lynch. Room after room, handshake after handshake, we laid out what we had built and where we believed it could go.

Our final stop was the Mandarin Hotel in San Francisco. As we wrapped up our last presentation, we received the call: our Initial Public Offering was oversubscribed. Investors wanted more shares than we had offered. With that single call, in that perfect moment, the three of us became multimillionaires.

What struck me was not just the money. For years, Chris and Bob had believed in me. Now the entire investment world believed in us. That was a different kind of validation, one I had never experienced before.

As the limousine rolled through downtown San Francisco, I remembered hot summer days in New Orleans spent digging pools. My coworkers from the pool company not only shared their lunches with me but also motivated me to aim higher. Those times were a mix of hardship and kindness, influencing my worldview. Even after many years, their support and encouragement remain with me.

At forty-three, I sat in the back of a limo, reflecting on my journey. After so many years of struggle, I had been making only $50,000 annually, had a credit limit of $500, and owed hundreds of thousands in high-interest debt. A decade after the Reunion Hall financial disaster at the World's Fair, I was still weighed down by that debt as I relocated from New Orleans to Texas, then to Florida.

Now, with one signature, I could settle it all. For the first time in a decade, the weight was gone. I was reclaiming my life and steering my own course.

That is why, when Outback finally went public, it was more than just a financial milestone. It was an emotional one. I had spent years working eighty to a hundred hours a week, building menus, training staff, and opening restaurants while carrying debt that never stopped growing. For the first time in my life, I was debt-free. Every early morning, every late night, every dollar I put toward that loan instead of toward my own comfort had finally paid off.

The risk we all took together had become the reward of a lifetime.

We arrived at the iconic Golden Gate Bridge. I asked the driver to open the sunroof, please. Then I stood up, the wind hitting my face, and looked out at the most beautiful bridge in the world.

I grabbed a bottle of champagne and popped the cork. It sprayed everywhere, soaking the roof, the seats, and my suit. The mist caught the late-afternoon sun through the sunroof, and for a second, the whole backseat glowed gold. I could not stop laughing. I told the driver I would cover the cleaning bill, but in that moment, nothing could diminish the joy I felt. My passage from debt to financial security had finally been achieved.

Ever since I saw a photo of the Golden Gate Bridge as a boy in Florida, I have been captivated by its grandeur, the scale of its engineering, and the boldness behind its creation. As the world's most photographed bridge, it made the ideal backdrop for celebrating this extraordinary June day.

After the champagne and the laughter, I settled back into the seat and let the silence take over. I wanted this moment to be mine alone. Not another handshake or presentation, but a private moment with every struggle, every failure, every small victory, and every dream I had carried since I was a teenager in Fort Lauderdale. Having grown up without a father and with a mother busy caring for five other children, I longed for that solitude, to sit quietly in the limo, savor my victory, and reflect on how much I had achieved.

We now had the fuel to build as many restaurants as we wanted.

The vision Chris, Bob, and I had shared from the beginning could become as big as we dared to make it.

This was not by luck. It was by choice. Every decision, every sacrifice, every moment I refused to quit had led me to this bridge, this sunset, this feeling that anything was possible.

I continued to reflect on the obstacles I overcame, the small victories won, the friendships I formed, the creation of the Bloomin' Onion, and the development of a restaurant empire. It felt like a near-religious experience.

When we got to the other side of the bridge, my limo driver asked, "Where do you want to go next?"

"Back across the Golden Gate," I said.

"Again?" he asked.

"And again," I said.

I never wanted the feeling to end. This exhilarating emotional high was a celebration of one chapter closing and another beginning in my life. With each crossing of that beautiful bridge, my excitement and sense of freedom increased. I felt unstoppable.

My time at Outback was never just about making money. I felt a deep sense of fulfillment from knowing we made a difference in people's lives. We offered opportunities by creating jobs, supporting education, and even aiding developing countries through our restaurant operations.

We also helped many people become millionaires, which was deeply fulfilling because it let them realize their dreams. We had a dedicated group of supporters, and that was very exciting. Even on the bridge, I thought I would stay at Outback for the rest of my life, even while pursuing other passions. I never wanted to leave.

That truth occupied my thoughts as my limousine crossed the Golden Gate Bridge. I sipped champagne and realized I had become a leader, no longer relying on a mentor. It became my responsibility to give back, a duty I accepted wholeheartedly. Over the years, I have given lectures at Wharton, generously supported numerous causes, assisted others with medical expenses, and always aimed to serve with true generosity. Giving back was not about appearances. It was the deepest obligation wealth could entail.

Then, on that beautiful San Francisco bridge, as the red-orange sunset blended into the Pacific and my thoughts raced for what felt like hours, I refocused on new challenges. In particular, I concentrated on the dream that had been stirring in me since I was a teenager.

My next step was clear: I was finally free to pursue polo with everything I had. Every effort and decision I had made in my life had led to this moment: the chance to play the game I loved at the highest level.

Sixteen

My Polo Career Begins

My son Chris once said, "Life's rules never applied to Dad. He always lived by his own terms. Nothing ever stood in his way."

This was not my first time in the saddle. Years earlier, while managing restaurants in New Orleans, I bought a paint horse from Phil for $800. Every weekend, I drove an hour across Lake Pontchartrain to a polo club in Folsom. With only one horse, they put me in the last chukker. I would wait through nine chukkers just to play one period at the end. Two hours of driving for seven minutes of polo. But I did it every chance I got. It kept the dream alive.

With Outback's success, I could finally train seriously.

My journey into real polo began in the fields behind my new house, riding Chiquita, a beautiful chestnut quarter horse mare I bought for fifteen thousand dollars. I rode her nearly every day, working to make her an extension of myself. I knew I was not prepared for a large, costly thoroughbred. Chiquita was just right, a partner suited to my beginner's level.

I was still learning the basics. Every morning, I would gallop from one end of the polo field to the other as fast as I could, the wind in my face, feeling like I was finally chasing the dream I had carried since that handshake with Phil. But the moment Chiquita stopped, I would pitch forward right over her neck and hit the ground hard. It happened again and again. Her ability to stop so quickly threw me forward, and I had no idea how to counter it.

After every fall, I would dust myself off and climb back on, wondering how many more times I could do it. My body ached. I went through bottles of Advil just to get through those early days. But I kept getting up. I kept riding. I refused to quit.

Finally, one of the skilled polo players walked over and watched me take another spill. He shook his head and said, "You are doing it all wrong."

"Kick your feet forward," he said. "Like on a motorcycle. You have to counterbalance. Put your feet far forward when you come to a stop so your shoulders go back. Your weight should always be on the horse's back, not the front."

I got up, tried it, and stayed on. Just like that. One small adjustment changed everything.

That was my first real lesson in polo. When you ride horses for pleasure, you gallop and gallop and rarely need to stop quickly. Polo is different. Polo demands quick stops, sharp turns, and sudden bursts of speed. The horse must become part of you, and you must learn to move with her.

Phil had told me the secret years earlier: hours in the saddle. The more you ride, the more comfortable you become. I learned to hold the reins in one hand and neck-rein Chiquita, teaching her to turn with pressure from my left hand. The right hand had to stay free for the mallet. I developed muscles I never knew I had, gripping the horse from my hips to my kneecaps, building strength in my inner thighs until I could hold on through anything.

Spending time with Chiquita strengthened my passion for polo and horses.

I love polo for several reasons: unlike football, basketball, or baseball, where I was not naturally talented, polo on horseback made me

Riding Chiquita.

feel like a genuine athlete. I have always longed for the camaraderie and unity found in team sports, which I lacked as a child. Polo introduced me to teamwork, showing that success requires everyone working together, not just individual effort. I truly felt like I was coming out of the dugout.

Even when I played tennis, I preferred doubles since it involved developing chemistry with a teammate to succeed. Although I was not initially an elite polo player, I excelled at forming effective teams. This was my strength. I could assemble one team roster, then create another, often leading the new team to outperform the previous one because I kept honing my ability to spot talent. From a team-building standpoint, polo resembles a complex chess game.

Polo offers a mental challenge as engaging as chess, requiring both the horse's physical athleticism and, to a lesser degree, the rider's. This distinctive mix, combined with the constant risk that a fall could be life-threatening or cause paralysis, generates a thrilling adrenaline rush. Together, these factors make polo my sport of choice.

As the world's oldest team sport, polo predates baseball by several centuries. Historians trace its origins to Persia (now Iran) around the sixth century B.C., where it began as a cavalry training exercise, especially for royal guards and elite soldiers. For the fiercely competitive tribesmen, polo matches, with as many as 100 players on each side, simulated the ferocity of actual battles.

Over the years, polo evolved into a Persian national sport, played primarily by the nobility. It was popular among the elite, with both men and women participating.

As trade and cultural exchanges flourished, the game spread from Persia to Arabia and eventually to Tibet, China, and Japan.

One of the notable stories in polo's history dates to 910, when Khitan Emperor Abaoji ordered that all players be executed after a relative's death in a match. This harsh reaction highlights polo's importance in imperial courts; it was more than just entertainment; it was an arena where reputations, alliances, and lives could be at stake.

Over thousands of years, as the game spread across nations, its rules and danger levels remained largely unchanged. Kings and princes experienced both victories and losses. King Charles III, then Prince of Wales, broke his arm, was knocked unconscious, and sustained numerous other injuries during his polo career. Prince William fell from his horse during a match, a reminder that polo makes no exceptions for royalty.

Today, the core skills needed to excel in polo are unchanged: razor-sharp hand-eye coordination, exceptional horsemanship, and, above all, unwavering courage and fearlessness.

Once you begin playing polo, you will quickly fall in love with it. Even my close friend, actor Tommy Lee Jones, has taken up the sport. His passion for polo is evident. The game fascinates him and many others, just as great things do. They play, and they want to play again. Polo is a sport that demands everything from its players but rewards them in return.

Polo is a challenging sport. Maintaining balance on the horse is difficult, especially when leaning out of the saddle to strike the ball with a mallet. Handling the ball is also tricky; it can be crushed under the horse's foot or bounce unpredictably, complicating aiming. It is uncommon to see the ball perfectly aligned for a shot.

I have seen players lift themselves entirely out of their saddles, supported solely by their kneecaps, to strike the ball while their horses gallop at full velocity. The athleticism required is impressive. The best players seem to perform miracles with the ball in the air, passing to teammates, shooting with precision, or defending with great skill.

Mastering the art of maneuvering the horse while playing the ball is essential, especially for preventing the opposing team from scoring.

My early days in Tampa, Florida, when I began as a partner at Outback Steakhouse, are unforgettable. The moment that stood out most was my first trip to the polo fields at Walden Lake in Plant City, just a short drive from Tampa. In that instant, I realized, "This is why I'm relocating. Now I understand why I'll be working a hundred hours a week." Chris Sullivan noticed my enthusiasm and said he saw the fire in my eyes.

My Outback partners had a different passion: golf. After we went public, Chris and Bob traveled the world to play on the best courses. In 1994, they decided to create their own masterpiece by purchasing a 312-acre site with Bob Merritt, Outback's CFO, just fifteen minutes from Outback's corporate headquarters in Tampa. Three years later, after extensive design and construction, they opened Old Memorial Golf Club.

Designed by Steve Smyers, the course skillfully blends the finest features of Scotland's seaside links with those of Australia's famous sandbelt courses. But Old Memorial is more than a remarkable layout; it celebrates traditions cherished by golf enthusiasts. Initially, the club was walk-only. Each player, as at Augusta National, was paired with a professional caddy in a traditional white jumpsuit, who shared inside knowledge and stories about the 7,389-yard course throughout the round. Winning the Outback lottery benefited everyone involved.

The success of Outback did not just shape my partner's golf-course business ventures; it also transformed my personal life.

The rise of Outback as a national icon allowed me to join the Tampa Polo Club and purchase more horses, strengthening my involvement in the sport. Club polo offers the flexibility to select your

With Tommy Lee Jones

level of competitiveness, much like pick-up basketball, serving as a way to develop my skills and relax after the demanding work of growing Outback. Over time, my polo skills consistently improved.

Even before we took Outback public, I knew I would become heavily involved in polo once I had the resources. I also knew I would apply the lessons I learned as one of Outback's co-founders to build a polo team.

Not long after that memorable day when I crossed the Golden Gate Bridge multiple times in a limousine, a true milestone in my life, I called my close friend Phil Heatley, now a lawyer in Houston. I never forgot the promise we made at sixteen: the one who achieved the greatest success and made it big would fund our polo team, while the other would manage it.

The moment had arrived for me to fulfill that promise I made long ago.

Phil, do you remember shaking hands when we were sixteen? That promise we made to each other?" He nodded. "I sure do." "Well, now is the time. I am honoring our pact," I said. "I want you as my polo manager."

As a criminal defense lawyer, he remained unconvinced. "I don't know," he admitted. "I already run my own law firm. Are you sure this Outback Polo team will succeed?" I reassured him it would. He needed more time to decide. I called him several more times, but he was not ready to commit. Finally, I made one last call.

"Phil, this is it," I said. "I'm not going to ask you again because I've got to move forward. I really want you to be our general manager. This is our dream. This is what we shook hands on when we were sixteen. We said that whichever of us hit it big would pay for our polo team, and the other would run it. Now we can live our dream. We can do everything we aspired to as teenagers. It is all here, sitting in front of us. If you do not take the job now, I will be forced to hire someone else. But I really want you. You are my best friend, and I know we will do some amazing things together.

My lobbying finally paid off. With his wife, Shelley, Phil agreed to relocate from Houston to Sarasota, a short drive south of Tampa, to become the general manager of Outback Polo. He bought a house near a polo field.

I wanted to share my success with others, especially Phil. Years ago, when I was digging pools in New Orleans, Phil figuratively pulled me out, introduced me to polo, and showed me what true friendship is.

Now it was my turn to return the favor: I was helping him out of a struggling law firm and changing the course of his life by giving him the gift of polo. Our roles had reversed, and I could not be happier to have Phil back in my daily life.

Early on, Phil said he was glad I was the first to hit it big because he doubted he would have been as generous. I believe he would have been. I have always felt that when you give freely, the kindness and love you share eventually come back to you. And you know what? They have.

Under Phil's leadership, Outback Polo assembled a talented team and quickly began winning tournaments across Florida. Our breakthrough came at the Gulfstream Polo Club, where we won the 1994 National 8-Goal Tournament trophy, a great start, even if it was not the U.S. Open.

Moving quickly from low-goal to medium-goal polo, we secured another national title, the 14-goal Copper Cup at Palm Beach Polo. I shared this victory with Phil, Boone Stribling, and Ricky Bostwick.

Low-goal, medium-goal, and high-goal describe a polo team's level of play.

Each player is assigned a handicap from minus-2 to 10 based on skill and experience, with only about two dozen players in the world holding the top rating at any given time. The four players' handicaps are added together to determine the team's total, and the higher the number, the more elite the competition.

By late 1994, Outback Polo was gaining momentum. In November, I traveled to Argentina, known for some of the world's best polo, where I hosted Alfonso Pieres. Alfonso and his brother Gonzalo both had a 10-goal handicap, and their La Espadaña team had won the Argentina Open six times. When I left Buenos Aires two weeks later, Alfonso had agreed to join Outback Polo the following month.

Bringing Alfonso onto our team was like signing Tom Brady as a free agent in 2020, an absolute game-changer. Thanks to his presence, Outback quickly became the dominant force in Sarasota polo, consistently defeating all our rivals. After just a few months with Alfonso, I was ready to move Outback into the high-goal polo circuit.

In the spring that followed, I had my first taste of high-goal polo at Palm Beach Polo, where I competed against Memo Gracida, an icon in the sport. Born in Mexico City to the celebrated Gracida polo family, Memo boasts an illustrious international career, including a record sixteen U.S. Open titles and twenty-one consecutive years as an American 10-goal player, more than any other. He is notably the only player ever inducted into the American Polo Hall of Fame while still competing.

When we first competed, Memo had recently won three straight U.S. Open titles and was seen as the Michael Jordan or Babe Ruth of polo.

As captain, Memo led Guy Wildenstein's Les Diables Bleus, which included 10-goal scorer Mike Azzaro, in the highly competitive 22-goal league. The match between Outback Polo and Les Diables Bleus was unforgettable. Instead of the standard six chukkers, the game ended in a tie and extended into triple overtime, with each additional chukker adding to the excitement, totaling three overtimes, a rare and exhilarating event.

Although we ultimately lost to Les Diables Bleus, our first game against their talented 10-goaler showed we could challenge him and his team. Even in defeat, I felt victorious because we proved we belonged on that field with the best.

Memo was so impressed with Outback Polo's performance that he called me afterward and invited me to join him on the field for a practice match. By the time it was over, I had already scored twelve goals. Let us just say I had a lot of help doing that.

Memo's record spoke volumes: as a proven leader, he had led teams such as Retama, Carter Ranch, and Les Diables Bleus to U.S. Open victories. I was convinced that for Outback Polo to move forward, Memo had to lead us.

At that point, I brought him on board for Outback Polo's U.S. Open team. My talent was to assemble great polo players who could work seamlessly together as a team.

"I managed the finances for the horses and polo," Phil Heatley shares. "Tim always told me, 'Phil, I don't want to know the bills. Don't tell me.' He'd make these bold deals, but they always turned out well. Tim is very skilled at making big decisions and making them quickly."

Memo was firm that we prepare for the Open by taking part in a lead-up tournament. As it turned out, our only option was the USPA Silver Cup, America's oldest tournament, dating back to 1900. The Silver Cup, along with the USPA Gold Cup and the Open, is among the most prestigious in American polo. Although joining such a prestigious event was a significant milestone for our new team, Memo, a veteran professional, saw it more as routine practice than a tough challenge.

We loaded our horses and drove from Florida to Norman, Oklahoma, home of the Silver Cup. Our team consisted of Memo, Tino Bourdieu, my long-time friend Phil Heatley, who served as both general manager and player, and me.

Unexpectedly, Memo's father was hospitalized in Mexico City. Despite this personal challenge, Memo demonstrated remarkable resilience. He led us to victory on the field and, between matches, flew home to support his father.

Despite Memo's thoughts being in Mexico, his legendary leadership carried us. We lined up: I at No. 1, Tino at 2, Memo at 3, and Phil playing Back.

Our opponents, Grant's Farm, organized by Andy and Billy Busch, were led by the formidable Hector Galindo, one of the world's best players. Still, Outback Polo proved unstoppable. We dominated the final from start to finish, never relinquishing our three- or four-goal lead and securing a decisive 12–9 victory.

We were on a high. After winning the Silver Cup, we celebrated with a meal at Outback in Norman, starting what would become a legendary winning streak. This streak of titles was something any corporate polo team in the country would envy, even well-established ones backed by companies like Chili's or Coca-Cola. For them, this would have been the peak of their history. However, my goal has always been clear: to make Outback Polo the gold standard organization not only in the United States but across the globe.

Our next major tournament, where we aim to defeat more giants: the U.S. Open.

The U.S. Open took place on Long Island, the very place I drove to from Twin Farms, Texas, thirty years ago, during the summer before my junior year in high school. Back then, with my friends Jeff and Johnny, I watched my first high-stakes professional polo matches. Although my passion for polo began earlier, in Fort Lauderdale, where I first experienced the sport, it was on Long Island that I encountered polo at a professional, intensely competitive level. Returning to Long Island underscored how pivotal those early experiences were in shaping the path my life would follow.

Knowing that Phil and I were returning to a place so meaningful in my life story, I invited Phil's dad, Bud Heatley, to join us. He was the first to introduce me to polo. Now, we were all together again, playing at Bethpage State Park, where Bud had competed in many matches decades ago.

To honor Bud, I had a custom-made Outback Polo letter jacket made for him, with "COACH" stitched beneath his name. Bud's early inspiration and support were crucial to my reaching the pinnacle of American high-goal polo. To symbolize how everything had come full circle, I brought along the magic saddle he had given me in my youth, which I later bought back from Bill Lund. This saddle remains, and always will be, among my most treasured possessions.

I was confident in our team and excited to pursue the dream that started when Phil took me to my first polo match as a teenager. Still, before facing our first opponent, I knew we needed to upgrade our lineup with genuine Open-caliber horses.

Not long after we arrived in New York, Memo took me aside and told me confidently that Guy Wildenstein was looking to sell his finest horses: twenty Thoroughbreds that had brought Les Diables Bleus victory in three U.S. Opens as well as the USPA Gold Cup. Memo asked if I wanted to buy them.

"Memo, if you think so, then let's do it," I said. "Buy all twenty of them."

Judging by the raised eyebrow look on Memo's face, I am guessing he had never seen a patron answer such a key question so quickly, so decisively, and so definitively. But to me, it was a no-brainer: I was going to do everything in my power to put us in the best possible position to succeed.

"Tim," Memo said to me, "you're the ultimate teammate."

On Outback's first Open team, Julio Arellano and Memo's brother Carlos joined Memo and me. At the time, most polo experts considered Carlos, who had surpassed Memo, as the world's top player. In 1994, just a year earlier, Carlos achieved the remarkable feat of winning polo's Triple Crown: the British Gold Cup, the U.S. Open, and the Argentina Open. His captivating presence on the field left spectators in awe.

Just days before the '95 Open, Carlos's luck took a turn for the worse. To prepare, we traveled from Long Island to Connecticut for a practice match against Pegasus at Peter Brant's club. Halfway through, an accidental collision between Benjamin Araya's horse and Carlos's mount caused Carlos's horse to lose balance and fall. It was a stark reminder of the ever-present risks in polo. Carlos, unfortunately, broke his right thumb in the incident.

Many teams would have withdrawn from the Open if they had lost their top player just days before it started. But I stayed firm: Outback Polo was going to play, even without Carlos. I had waited twenty years to compete in the Open, and after the injury, I told Memo we were moving forward, that we were going to compete, and that I needed him to find a replacement, a very talented one, fast. He heard me loud and clear.

Having played high-goal polo for over twenty years across five continents, Memo had the sport's most extensive Rolodex. Simply put, if you were involved in polo, Memo knew you and had your contact information. Within minutes of being asked to find a substitute for his brother, Memo was already calling around the globe, determined to secure a 10-goal player to fill Carlos's place on Outback Polo and there were only 10 players at the 10-goal handicap to choose from.

Memo's pitch was both compelling and straightforward: this is an incredible opportunity. He highlighted our impressive Silver Cup win and emphasized that Outback is currently the favorite to win the Open. Memo also assured potential candidates that they would inherit Carlos's string of top-tier horses, alleviating any concerns about the quality of the horses.

It did not take long for Memo to catch his target. Sebastian Merlos, a young Argentine 10-goaler, seized the opportunity and quickly headed to the airport in Buenos Aires for a flight to New York. We had our man, despite the tight schedule. He caught his flight the night before the tournament was set to start.

Eleven hours later, on the morning of our first match, I arranged for a car to pick up Sebastian from LaGuardia Airport as soon as he cleared customs. He was driven straight to Greenwich to face off against Russo and Pepe Heguy's team. To me, it almost felt like divine intervention, a sign from above that we were destined for greatness and that we would not be denied.

None of us had ever played together before, but you would not have known it. Our teamwork was effortless; we moved as one, entirely in sync. We dominated, overwhelming our opponents like seasoned giants facing a team of rookies. Sebastian, fresh off an international flight, showed no trace of jet lag; he was sharp and fast on Carlos's superb horses. Julio, motivated by Sebastian and Memo, delivered an outstanding performance. My own game and confidence grew stronger with each chukker. Just as a rising tide lifts all boats, my teammates' world-class talent inspired me to reach a dream level of play. This was not a dream; it was the reality I had worked my whole adult life to achieve.

With Bud still by my side, cheering us on after all these years as a father-like figure I longed to make proud, we swept through the preliminary matches, winning every one with ease. From my first days learning polo at sixteen on Bud's farm in El Paso, reaching the final of the U.S. Open was my greatest dream. Now, it was within my grasp.

In the semifinals, Cellular One had no chance. We annihilated Cellular One in the semifinals, obliterating them 18–4.

Memo set the tone for the championship: play fast, hard, and open polo. We followed his lead, unleashing relentless hit-and-run tactics throughout all six chukkers, never easing up. Julio delivered a career-best performance at No. 1, while Sebastian played outstanding twelve-goal polo at No. 2. Memo was flawless, converting every penalty shot. I pushed myself to the limit, seized my moment, rode fiercely, and defended our goal against top-tier opponents: Mariano Aguerre, Adolfo Cambiaso, and Peter Brant. From the outset, White Birch was overwhelmed. We triumphed, 15–6.

When the final horn sounded, an overwhelming wave of happiness washed over me. We had just secured our first U.S. Open Championship. A lifelong dream was now reality. The celebration that followed seemed to move in slow motion, like a vivid dream.

I remember riding toward the pony lines and seeing Bud. He was wearing his custom Outback Polo jacket, the one with "COACH" stitched beneath his name. I have never seen a man jump so high. He was leaping up and down, tears streaming down his face.

He ran toward me, shouting, "We did it!"

Then he caught himself and said, "You did it. Congratulations."
I said, "No, Bud. We did it."

Those words meant everything to him. I could see it in his eyes. Here was the man who had handed me a polo saddle thirty years ago and told me to put it to good use. The man who had painted a path for a skinny, broke kid from Fort Lauderdale and given him the optimism to chase something that seemed impossible. Now, in front of all the old polo families who had known him over the years, the Phipps, the Graces, and so many others, we had done it together.

What I did not know then was that this would be the last time Bud would ever coach a team. His mind was beginning to fade, with the early signs of dementia setting in. But on that day, he was fully present, fully alive, fully in the moment with me. It was the perfect ending to a thirty-year journey that began on his farm in Texas.

After all those years of hard work, I finally achieved it all: discovering my Velcro, achieving financial success, and winning the U.S. Open. What made it even sweeter was having Bud as my coach and my best friend, Phil, by my side. Life could not have been better.

Now it was truly time to celebrate! I had brought my yacht up to New York in case we secured a victory so we could celebrate around Manhattan. After our win, I gathered the team, along with our families and friends, for a cruise on Long Island Sound from Oyster Bay docks. The memories of that afternoon remain vivid: hugs, high-fives, laughter, toasts, and champagne sipped from the U.S. Open trophy as we circled the Statue of Liberty. I never do anything halfway, and this celebration was the ultimate expression of that.

Growing up in Fort Lauderdale, my family and I often found ourselves stuck in traffic as drawbridges lifted to let large boats pass on our way to the beach. I was mesmerized by the people aboard those massive vessels and wondered what their lives were like. Years later, I found myself aboard one of those very boats with my siblings, feeling deeply loved and fulfilled.

It was one of those moments that made me stop, reflect, and savor every detail. Taking a quick break from the party, I looked out over the water at the towering Manhattan skyline, the buildings rising so high they seemed to scrape the sky. When I turned back to see my friends and teammates, a deep sense of gratitude washed over me. I truly felt like the luckiest person alive.

Here I was, an entrepreneur in a land full of endless opportunities. I was not only turning my dreams into reality, but also helping others achieve theirs, which made the experience even more meaningful. After all, the most memorable moments in life are not truly special unless shared with loved ones. I did exactly that, and it was beautiful. Truly beautiful.

Outback Polo was the new team challenging established giants, and we were on the verge of building our own dynasty. I credit much of our early success, including our first U.S. Cup win, to the respect I showed our team captains, starting with Memo on Long Island. This respect underscored a key lesson from my Outback partners: always share the spotlight and let others succeed without interference.

Memo observed, "Even though 1995 was Tim's first Open, he conducted himself like a seasoned pro. He had complete trust in my judgment and gave me full authority over strategic decisions during matches. Tim never second-guessed my calls. Outback was his team, but he didn't try to act as a field general, as some patrons do. He genuinely wanted to win, and that kind of commitment is crucial at the highest level of polo."

But our journey had only just begun.

Seventeen

Rising to the Top of the Polo World

The roar of victory from our first U.S. Open had barely faded when the next challenge appeared on the horizon. Success in polo, much like in life, is never static; it requires you to keep proving yourself. Outback Polo quickly rose from obscurity to claim the top spot in the sport, but now we faced a new reality: defending our crown. The days of being the underdog were gone. We were no longer the surprise team that stunned the giants; we had become the giants, the team everyone wanted to beat.

Six months after winning our first U.S. Open title, Outback Polo again delivered a strong performance. The United States Polo Association moved the Open from Long Island to South Florida and shifted the schedule from fall to spring. As a result, we were ready to defend our title at Palm Beach Polo just 180 days after our Long Island victory, celebrating like rock stars on a yacht beneath the Statue of Liberty.

We were prepared for the challenge, poised to be the team with a bullseye on our jerseys. No longer the unknown underdog, we had become the heavyweight everyone aimed to defeat. This time, the team included Memo, Mike Azzara, Vale Aguilar, and me.

A new face appeared on the sideline, one who would play a crucial role for us: Joe Barry, our new coach. As a player, Joe had multiple U.S. Open titles, and I wanted his experience to guide us through the challenging task of repeating our success. In 1977 and '79, he teamed up with Memo for Retama and clinched U.S. Open titles both years, being well acquainted with Memo and his skills. Joe's passion and wise words would be vital to our progress.

During our first match, we experienced early struggles. Our teamwork was disorganized, resembling four individuals rather than a united team. We needed a leader to guide us and improve our coordination. After falling behind midway through the game, Joe stepped up to address us.

"Guys, you've been given a great opportunity," he said. "The U.S. Open is the greatest tournament in the world, and what are you doing? You're treating it like a regular match."

As he spoke, tears welled in Joe's eyes. We all knew what a fierce champion he was, and seeing him heartbroken by how we were playing was exactly what we needed. His emotion awakened the sleeping giant. He finished his powerful speech by telling us to go out and play like the champions we are.

We entered the field as a revitalized team, reigniting the same magic from six months earlier and transforming into the well-oiled machine we once were on Long Island. We easily won our first-round game and dominated every following match, regaining our reputation as heavyweight champions. We were unstoppable, reminiscent of Mike Tyson at his prime.

The final felt more like a celebration than a competitive game; it was a joyful event. We scored early and often, defeating Casa Manila 16–9 to secure our second Open title in under a year. This time, in-

Second U.S Open Championship in a row. Vale Aguilar, Memo Gracida, Mike Azzaro, and Coach Joe Barry.

stead of taking the yacht to sail Long Island Sound, I took the team to the Bahamas to celebrate a truly exceptional milestone: Outback's impressive ascent to the pinnacle of American polo.

Memo played at his peak. Sitting with cocktails on a Bahamas beach, he turned to me and said, "That was the best Open team I have ever been part of." As the waves gently hit the sand, I realized: in all my sports career, this would be the highest compliment I would ever receive.

After winning back-to-back U.S. Open championships in 1995

The Silver Cup.

Christening the yacht.

and 1996, I faced a decision. I had achieved what I set out to do, reaching heights I never imagined possible. Rather than risk seeing my performance decline, I chose to retire while still at the top of my game.

I sold my entire string of horses, including those from Guy Wildenstein and Galen Weston, to fellow polo enthusiast John Goodman, a Texas-based businessman and founder of the International Polo Club Palm Beach. Memo Gracida, who had led us to victory, joined Goodman's Isla Carroll team. In 1997, I watched from the

Trophy in hand.

sidelines as they defeated White Birch 10-6 to win the U.S. Open.

But as Memo performed on the field and relentlessly dominated the competition, I felt a deep stirring in my soul: I knew I had to return to the game and play my part. It is an understatement to say that watching from the sidelines did not suit me at all. I had to find a way to rejoin the game.

Later that year, during the Argentine Triple Crown, I received a call from Adolfo Cambiaso.

Adolfo and I had met in 1995 during the U.S. Open final on Long

Island, where Outback beat White Birch. Adolfo was unhappy with White Birch, despite being on a talented team. The team's captain, Mariano Aguerre, made all decisions, insisting on his way or the highway. This did not sit well with Adolfo, who saw himself as a leader, a cavalryman rather than a foot soldier. Simply put, Adolfo was not built to follow orders.

I was surprised when, during our conversation, he asked whether I was interested in having him assemble a team for Outback. I agreed immediately.

Deep down, I knew that a passion for polo was still part of my DNA. More importantly, Adolfo was a once-in-a-generation phenomenon, a Halley's Comet lighting the sky, a player whose skill surpassed even that of the great Memo.

At just 19, Adolfo achieved Argentina's prestigious Triple Crown by winning the Tortugas Open, the Hurlingham Open, and the Argentine Open. He was later awarded a 10-goal rating, establishing himself as one of the world's top polo players. No one in Argentine polo history had ever become a 10-goaler at such a young age, making his achievement even more extraordinary.

Despite his many triumphs, one achievement was missing from his résumé: winning a U.S. Open. In fact, the worst defeat Adolfo ever faced was at the hands of Outback Polo in the 1995 U.S. Open final. Adolfo understood what we were capable of, and he wanted to join our team. He had no idea, but he was asking the perfect person to be his patron. I have always been fascinated by disruptors, and Adolfo was precisely one of them.

Peggy Guggenheim, George Biel, and Warren Leruth, each of whom has profoundly influenced my life, share a common trait. They were driven overachievers committed to excellence, believing no mountain was insurmountable and no obstacle too formidable. Their goal was to improve on what already existed, striving not just for a better version but for the best. Their relentless pursuit was perfection.

Adolfo's dedication to discovering the world's finest horses matched Peggy's passion for curating one of the most remarkable modern art collections, George's commitment to establishing the premier casual dining experience in America, and Warren's drive to uncover extraordinary flavors.

All four were relentless, gritty fighters, ingenious and hardworking. Driven by an unwavering pursuit of greatness, their internal motors always operated at full throttle.

My own drive was ignited by Corky Linfoot, who sparked my inner fire with a single remark. A two-time U.S. Open champion and an exceptional coach, Corky understands polo as well as anyone in the game. I was in Santa Barbara, his hometown, at the 1997 Pacific Coast Open when he said something that resonated with me. "You won two U.S. Opens with Memo," he said. "But the real test, Tim, is if you can beat Memo."

That was all I needed to hear. The gauntlet had been thrown down. Challenge accepted. Game on.

In 1998, after a one-year break from the sport, I decided to get back into the sport that I love, and Outback Polo resumed its pursuit of the U.S. Open. Alongside Adolfo, our team included his close friend from Cañuelas, Lolo Castagnola, and John Gobin.

Adolfo and Lolo brought seventeen of their own horses from Argentina, marking the beginning of our extensive effort to rebuild the stable with Thoroughbreds carefully sourced by Phil from across the country and around the world.

That year's U.S. Open took us to the semifinals. Our opponent: the Isla Carroll team, led by Memo Gracida, the man who had captained us to two consecutive championships. Playing alongside him was his brother Carlos, another world-class talent. The match took place in South Florida, on the field behind what would become my home.

How strong was my desire to win? The day before the semifinal, I promised Adolfo a $50,000 bonus if we beat Memo, sending a message to Corky Linfoot that once I focus on something, nothing can stop me.

But Adolfo's response took me by surprise. "Tim, if you've got $50,000 to spend, then spend it on a great horse," he said. "You will own it. I will ride it. And hopefully it will carry us to victory tomorrow."

Phil and I searched extensively for an elite horse, but none were available for sale. During the semifinal, we lacked fresh horses, yet our team competed with heart, grit, and strong resolve. Despite our efforts, it was not enough, and we were defeated by Memo and Carlos.

Before winning the U.S. Open trophy.

Yes, I was disappointed, but I am not someone who dwells on defeat. I have never been that way in any venture in my life. The loss only fueled my desire to beat Memo. I immediately decided to get more horses for the Outback Polo team.

That summer, Adolfo called me from England. Kerry Packer was shutting down Ellerston's operations in England, and he had two hundred horses for sale. I told Adolfo to pick the ones he wanted, and we ended up buying forty of Kerry's best horses for $50,000 each. We transported them to Spain, where we competed for both

The USPA Open trophy and its 103 championship medallions.

the Spanish Silver and the Spanish Gold Cups.

With our new roster of elite horses and skilled players, we remained unbeatable, securing victory in both tournaments.

On a day off from the Gold Cup, I took my fourteen-year-old son, Chris, to watch a bullfight. Locals insisted that experiencing this tradition was essential to understanding their culture. In the 1990s, bullfighting remained deeply embedded in Spanish society, a celebrated spectacle that drew crowds across the country.

As a polo player, I was fascinated by the roots of equestrian tradition, bullfighting on horseback, which originated as training for mounted warriors and remains a highly dangerous display of horsemanship in Spain. This form of bullfighting involved a rider guiding the horse as the bull charged and inserting banderillas into the bull's back. A single mistake or hesitation could result in the rider being gored or trampled. When the bull reached its limit, the rider would dismount and confront the animal on foot, increasing the danger.

I was so captivated that the very next day, Chris and I visited the ranch of one of Spain's most famous bullfighters, Álvaro Domecq Romero, who is also considered the world's most famous equestrian. Soon, I found myself in the practice ring, jousting with smaller bulls on horseback. The goal was to assess the bulls' bravery and determine whether, when they matured, they were worthy of fighting in a large arena before a large crowd.

"The bulls are running at my dad at about 25 to 30 miles per hour," Chris recalled. "From a distance, it looks like they are coming right at you. You do not know until the last two or three feet if it is going to miss you. It is a test of your courage. You are supposed to stand there and hold your ground and hope the bull keeps moving past you. But when you are new at it, like my dad, it is like, 'Oh shit!' Your human instincts kick in. But in practice, my dad did fine."

Chris continued:

"So my dad goes out there the next day at the arena in front of a vast crowd, and he does it perfectly two or three times. He stands his ground and shows his bravery. Once a professional bullfighter does this, he walks away, showing that he owns the bull, and he waves to the crowd. Well, that is what my dad does.

As he turned away and looked at the audience, he saw someone in our group's eyes widen, and she suddenly yelled. There was a bull charging right at him. My dad is not a real runner. And the bull pinned him against the wall and was about to gore him. But luckily, he just got bruised. I mean, he was all black and blue.

But that is not the end of the story. My dad, being my dad, asked a professional bullfighter for his red cape. He said he was going back out there. And that is what he did: he fought that bull one more time as if to say, 'You are not going to beat me.' And that bull did not. It was just another one of my dad's great adventures."

That fearless spirit seemed to follow us everywhere, whether in the ring or on the field. As horsemen, Adolfo and I were always searching for the best, and it was during our time in Spain that we discovered ourselves captivated by another breed of champions.

Two horses caught Adolfo's attention: Thoroughbreds named Edna and Fogata. Adolfo told me they were the best horses he had ever seen. It took me less than a second to reply: "Buy them both immediately, no matter the cost."

Adolfo then called Glen Gilmore, and together they made a deal, one that would have far-reaching repercussions for the entire sport of polo.

Edna was no ordinary mare. She made Adolfo unstoppable. With her beneath him, he achieved a level of speed, agility, and precision the sport had never seen. In polo, 10 goals is perfection, the highest possible rating. Adolfo on Edna played at a 12-goal level, literally off the charts, cementing his place as the best player in the world.

The following year, Outback Polo dominated the 1999 U.S. high goal season with tournament wins at the United States Polo Association Gold Cup in Boca Raton and the U.S. Open in Palm Beach. Adolfo, Lolo, Jeff Blake, and I won the final of the Open 13–9 over a strong Pony Express team that included Bautista and Gonzalo Heguy, Nic Roldan, and Bob Daniels.

Building on an incredible streak in the U.S., our momentum carried us across the Atlantic. Although relocating our entire operation to Spain was challenging, we relied on the confidence and experience we gained back home. Our efforts paid off with late-summer wins at the Spanish Silver and Gold Cups in Sotogrande, making the season unforgettable.

The highlight of that incredible year, a year I will always cherish, came in the final moments of the Spanish Gold Cup. Teams from Dubai, Australia, and around the world competed for the title. But none could beat Outback. Adolfo, Gonzalita Pieres, Alex Figueras, and I headed to the championship match, where we faced a French team called Calandracas.

Late in the game, with the score tied, a penalty was called on Calandracas. The pressure mounted. The crowd held its breath. I rode out on Michelita, one of my all-time favorite mares, to take the shot. Everything I had worked for came down to this.

What a moment it was. By this stage in my polo career, I had

Chris Gannon, Alvaro Domecq Romero, and Tim Gannon on horseback in Spain.

already won the U.S. Open three times, but this was something else: the world stage and a shot at a solid-gold trophy. In many ways, my entire life had led to this moment.

Clearing my mind, I focused on the ball and prepared for the backswing. Michelita approached perfectly, allowing me to deliver a confident, solid strike. That penalty point paved the way, and Outback Polo defeated Calandracas to win the Spanish Gold Cup.

Outback Polo's victory over Calandracas was our fourth international tournament win of the season. In recognition, Rolex named Outback Polo the number one polo team worldwide in 1999. I felt my journey was complete, and a boy from New Orleans who once dug pool ditches had reached the top of the world.

During our time in Sotogrande, I spotted a familiar face in the crowd. I could not place her at first, but something stirred my memory. She was watching the match intently, seated among friends from

With Phil, hoisting the Silver Cup in Spain.

With the Queen of Spain after winning the Silver Cup.

Riding out before the crowd at Soto Grande.

Championship celebration after winning the Gold Cup.

India's polo aristocracy.

After the match, she approached me.

"Are you not that young man from New Orleans who lent me a case of champagne glasses?" she asked.

The memory came flooding back. Thirty years earlier, in 1978, I was running Stephen and Martin's restaurant in New Orleans when a striking woman walked through the door. She had long black silk hair that fell to her waist, wore a beautiful sari, had a diamond in her nose, and wore a red dot on her forehead. I thought I had been taken to Indian heaven.

She had asked to borrow a case of champagne glasses. Without hesitation, I went to the storage room, retrieved them, and loaded them into her car. A week later, she returned the glasses and asked what she owed me. I told her nothing. They were a gift.

She was puzzled. She had mistaken my restaurant for Martin Wine Cellar, around the corner. I told her I was glad she had stopped at the wrong place.

We became friends. Her name was Yashodhara Raje Scindia, a princess of the Scindia dynasty of Gwalior, one of India's most powerful princely states. Polo's deepest roots are in India, where Maharajas played against each other for centuries before the sport spread to England and then to America. The Scindia family remains deeply connected to the sport, and I loved hearing her stories about the royal polo traditions.

I told her that one day I would become a great polo player and compete at the highest levels of the game. She smiled politely and whispered, "Good luck with that." I was running a 100-seat restaurant. The road ahead was long.

We lost touch over the years. And now here she was, standing before me in Spain.

"You have done well," she said. "I am very proud."

Thirty years after I made my promise in that small New Orleans restaurant, I had kept my word. And someone who had been there at the beginning was there to see it.

That reunion in Sotogrande reminded me of something I had always believed: the best moments in life come back to the people around you.

Adolfo understood this better than anyone, and he has always emphasized that what truly sets Outback apart is not the horses or the trophies, but how everyone is treated, including players, grooms, veterinarians, and assistants. No one is left out. We are all part of one team. This was not a formal policy. It was simply his belief about how things should be.

He often illustrates this with a story from Sotogrande that he loves to tell.

"One morning," Adolfo recalls, "Tim gathered everyone and laid four sets of keys on the table: a Porsche, a motorcycle, a regular car, and a bicycle lock. He told us that whoever woke up first would get first pick."

"The early riser chose the Porsche. The motorcycle went next. Then the car, and Tim usually ended up with the bicycle lock," Adolfo says, laughing.

In truth, I never wanted the Porsche, the motorcycle, or the car. What mattered most to me was the scene I saw every morning: my team laughing, competing over something trivial, simply enjoying each other's company. A simple, fun game with a set of keys.

The most important thing is the team's happiness, above all else. That same culture guided us through everything we accomplished in Spain that season.

The motto of Outback Polo became "Intimidate, Dominate, Celebrate." And that is precisely what we did, again and again.

It is hard to express just how far I have come in life, but Chris Sullivan captured it perfectly:

"Here's a guy so down on his luck he had to sell a polo saddle just to buy gas. Ten years later, Outback Polo is the top team in the world. That's Tim. He's a true bigtime thinker, passionate about life, and incredibly generous. His success is no accident."

I often tell young people: If there is one thing you should believe in, it is yourself. I have always done so, no matter my circumstances, whether I was broke or tying steel while building swimming pools in New Orleans.

Always believe. Always work. Always dream.

The trophies kept coming, the victories piling up. But somewhere along the way, I learned what truly matters: success is not what you win for yourself. It is what you help others win. That principle has driven me ever since.

*Charging forward in Outback
polo action.*

Tim and Phil Heatley share a smile on the polo grounds.

A tough moment during a match.

Fist bump on horseback after a play.

Full backswing during a match.

Charging downfield.

On horseback.

Gold Cup action at Sotogrande, Spain.

The Outback team between chukkers. Chris among the players.

Wearing number 1 against White Birch.

After a match in Wellington.

Eighteen

The Power of Sharing

It is one thing to live out your dreams and see them unfold as you once imagined. But trust me: the most significant moments in life happen when you help others reach their goals and aspirations. That is true fulfillment. How can I serve others? This is a question I have always asked myself. In answering it, I realized I have taken many people along on adventures they likely would never have experienced on their own.

Chris Sullivan first introduced me to the concept of deep sharing when he invited me to join him, Bob, and Trudy as the founding team of Outback Steakhouse. The details are already part of this story: my financial struggles, selling my polo saddle for gas money to get to Tampa, and staying at Bob's house because I could not afford a hotel. But the moment that still leaves me in awe was when our attorney said I needed $10,000 in cash to become a partner.

Without hesitation, Chris pulled out his checkbook, wrote the check, and told the attorney, "Tim is in."

That single act changed everything. Without Chris's faith in me that day, none of this would have happened, no Outback, no success, no polo championships. Others may have recognized my abilities, but Chris believed in my potential more than anyone else. He bet on me when it mattered most. Chris truly exemplifies deep loyalty and genuine friendship.

What made Chris exceptional was not just that initial act of generosity. It was how he continued to protect me over the years that followed.

When I joined Outback, I was nearly $500,000 in debt. I owed over $250,000 at 18% interest to Hibernia National Bank in New Orleans for the World's Fair project, and a much larger $200,000 debt to the IRS. Although the World's Fair made a profit and that profit paid off a separate bank loan, I never considered those payments personal income because I never actually received the money; it went directly to pay the bank loan. I was naive to assume that. The IRS took a different view, claiming its share of the income I never actually touched.

The IRS rarely negotiates. They can garnish your wages, seize your assets, and put liens on everything you own. That kind of debt does not just go away. Worse, it would have disqualified me from taking Outback public. Everything we had built could have collapsed due to my oversight.

I did not fully understand how powerful the IRS was until one Friday afternoon. After receiving my payroll check, I went to the bank, hoping to keep just $100 in cash. The bank informed me that the IRS had notified them: all funds deposited into my account would go directly to the IRS. Every dollar.

I went back to Outback and spoke with our financial officer, only to learn that he had been notified as well. Any funds that came to me, whether payroll, loans, or any other payments, had to go to the IRS first. I was locked out. No payroll. No loans. No cash of any kind. I could not cover my own living expenses.

That was when I appealed to Chris Sullivan. He did not hesitate. "I will handle this," he said. Chris met with the IRS on my behalf, and within a week, the crisis was resolved by selling some of my stock. But that was the longest week of my life, spent with no cash, no credit card, and no resources.

Understanding the depth of that debt was a humbling challenge. I could not see my first real penny until it was cleared.

As we prepared to go public, the IRS debt had to be paid first. You cannot take a company public with that kind of problem on your record.

I will never forget his kindness and his ability to solve a problem that seemed immense to me, one I had no idea how to fix on my own. Chris had a soft spot for people whose problems were not brought on by recklessness or bad character. Mine was simply inexperience. He gave me room to grow.

Chris's generosity taught me something that would shape the rest of my life: the power of sharing. What he gave me, I wanted to share with others.

The defining moment came at the 2000 U.S. Open, a remarkable achievement just six years after Outback Polo's founding. In that short span, we became the world's number-one polo team. We entered the tournament as defending champions, determined to win again.

Adolfo, true to form, assembled an incredible team: Lolo Castagnola, Dale Schwetz, and me. With this lineup, we felt unstoppable, like mighty lions of polo.

But we had a problem: we did not work well together in the field. That became clear during the lead-up tournaments to the U.S. Open. We lost our first game in the USPA Gold Cup to a talented Coca-Cola team, which moved us to the losers' bracket for the rest of the tournament.

To understand Adolfo, it is essential to recognize how crucial chemistry is to him. He envisions a team functioning seamlessly, with players anticipating each other's actions. However, at that time, we were disorganized, out of sync, and far from achieving our full potential.

This is why I chose Adolfo as our leader; he had a knack for selecting players that matched his polo style. Despite our challenges, I was committed to giving Adolfo full control over the Outback Polo team. I never doubted him, understanding that doubts could spread among the team and undermine their confidence. Athletes need self-belief to perform at their best. When Adolfo left White Birch, I made a promise to support him, and I was determined to keep it.

When the 2000 U.S. Open started, we lost our first game. After the match, Adolfo and I sat down in my barn for a heart-to-heart talk.

"We have no chance like this," Adolfo said.

Adolfo thought over my offer, pacing back and forth with his hands on his hips, resembling a philosopher lost in thought. His next words caught me completely off guard.

"I am going to replace Dale with Sunny Hale," Adolfo declared. "She is the best 4-goaler in Wellington."

Right before my eyes, this bold Argentine executed a groundbreaking move no one in polo saw coming: he was adding a woman to a U.S. Open team, giving Sunny a real chance to make history. At that point, she ranked higher than 96% of all players worldwide, including men. No woman had ever been on a U.S. Open-winning team.

There was one problem. Dale was a 5-goaler, and Sunny was rated at four goals. To keep our team handicap balanced, we needed a 2-goaler. That meant I could step aside. This did not matter to me. What mattered was giving our team the best chance to win, not protecting my ego. So even though I was the team sponsor, I volunteered to sit out and watch from the sidelines.

It was obvious to me who should take my place: my lifelong best friend, Phil Heatley.

Over thirty years ago, Phil first introduced me to polo when he invited me to Twin Farms at sixteen. Since then, my relationship with his family has grown stronger. I am now the godfather to his daughters, Hayley and Lindsay. His father, Bud Heatley, has fueled my adventurous side and broadened my perspectives beyond Fort Lauderdale. Bud has always played a fatherly and mentoring role in my life.

The Heatley family has significantly impacted my life over the years, shaping who I am more than anyone else.

I wanted to return the favor to Phil. He managed every aspect of the team: purchasing the horses, arranging transportation, hiring grooms, and handling all the details that contribute to a successful team. As our general manager, he had been present at every victory, but always from the sidelines. He had never played in a U.S. Open-winning team before. That was about to change.

Right in front of Adolfo, I picked up the phone. My heart pounding, I dialed Phil's number.

"Phil, you are going in for me," I told him. "You are playing in the U.S. Open."

Phil was shocked, but there was no time to process it. Our next match was the following day. No time to train. No time to prepare. He would have to step onto the field and play in the U.S. Open with less than 24 hours' notice. Everything depended on him.

Our opponents never saw it coming. The new lineup of Adolfo, Lolo, Sunny, and Phil proved unstoppable. Sunny and Phil breathed new life into our team. They secured five consecutive wins before beating Everglades 11-8 in the final, earning Outback Polo's fourth U.S. Open title.

I credited Adolfo because his lineup change transformed a struggling team into one that played with grace, determination, and unity. The team went from faltering to flawless. But after our final victory, Adolfo credited someone else: Sunny Hale, the first woman to win the U.S. Open.

Gold Cup celebration, Boca Raton.

"Sunny might be rated four goals, but she has a 10-goal polo mind," Adolfo said.

I could not have said it better myself. Sunny possessed the skills of a 10-goal player, including the ability to control the ball and mark her opponent effectively. Her all-around ability, combined with Phil's strong defensive performance, was crucial to our success.

On the night we claimed the title, we celebrated like always—without limits. However, this time, it felt different. We toasted a woman's outstanding performance and my best friend's stellar defense. Seeing Phil bask in the praise that evening, I felt unparalleled happiness. That is when it finally dawned on me:

It is always far more satisfying to give than to receive.

In the following season, Adolfo and I renewed our efforts. I chose to step back from playing in the Open to allow my seventeen-year-old son, Chris, to take my position. He had spent years observing polo from the sidelines, soaking in every aspect of the game.

Now, Chris had the opportunity to embark on an unforgettable adventure. Alongside Adolfo, Fabio Diniz, and Santiago Chavanne, Outback Polo secured its fifth U.S. Open title in seven years.

Seeing my son win his first U.S. Open title made me feel like the proudest father in the world.

Outback Polo's 2001 U.S. Open team was, without question, the best foursome we ever put together. It was not only well-balanced but also the strongest overall. It did not hurt that every member of the team was either a teenager or in their twenties. That youth served us exceptionally well.

Memo was the first to explain to me why younger players are so valuable to a team. In 1995, while we were putting together our U.S. Open roster, we needed a player with four goals. I suggested bringing in an experienced pro, someone with 8, 9, or 10 goals at their peak, with plenty of high-goal experience. Memo immediately dismissed this idea.

"No, Tim. You want someone who's just starting out, not an old pro on the decline," Memo said. "I can help a youngster play two goals better than their handicap. You watch. They improve so quickly during the tournament. They listen. They're not set in their ways."

As always, Memo was correct. We selected a very young Julio Arellano. Two weeks later, we won our first U.S. Open championship. That approach stayed with me throughout my polo career and was a key factor in making the 2001 team the most dominant in Outback Polo history. The other reason? Adolfo Cambiaso captained that team without compensation. The story behind why he did that starts a year earlier.

In August 2000, I made a pivotal decision that would alter the history of polo.

That summer, Adolfo's nine-year partnership with Ellerstina came to an end. History was repeating itself. Just as he had left White Birch in 1995, Adolfo was not built to follow orders. After winning the Triple Crown with Ellerstina in 1994, he wanted what no organization had given him: complete control.

Now he was starting fresh, co-founding La Dolfina with Bartolomé Castagnola in his hometown of Cañuelas. But just before the Argentine Open at Palermo, he faced a serious problem: he did not have enough horses to compete.

The polo world was not silent about it. Gonzalo Pieres, the man who had built Ellerstina, told the Argentine press that Adolfo was coming to the field with an empty halter. It was meant as a verdict. No horses. No organization. Nothing. Just ambition and a name.

When I learned of this, I immediately told Adolfo, "Take any of my horses you want."

He asked, "Tim, what do you mean?"

I said, "Any of my horses you think are good enough for Palermo, take them to Argentina and play them in the Triple Crown."

He hesitated, "But Tim…"

I insisted, "No buts, Adolfo. They are yours to keep."

Adolfo selected seven of my finest horses and flew them to Argentina. Usually, the best horses move from Argentina to America. This time, the journey was reversed.

That season, La Dolfina took the field for the first time. A brand-new team, with horses that had played in Florida six weeks earlier. They reached the semifinals at Tortugas, won the championship at Hurlingham, and played in the final at Palermo. It was not a beginning. It was a declaration.

None of it would have happened without those seven horses.

It was not a business decision. It was an act of friendship.

I did not realize I was funding the birth of a dynasty. I was simply supporting a friend as he pursued his dream. Two years later, Adolfo led La Dolfina to its first Argentine Open title. Since then, La Dolfina has won thirteen more titles, including eight consecutive wins from 2013 to 2020. It became the most dominant team in modern polo history.

Unlike typical sponsor-captain relationships, which are purely professional, ours was different. Outback Polo's success proves it. After I gifted Adolfo those horses, he returned to Palm Beach and captained Outback for free.

Having the world's greatest polo player on your side is remarkable. Having him compete without pay because he believes in you, as you believe in him? That is priceless.

The 2001 U.S. Open team at Outback Polo was united by genuine care for each other. That made us unbeatable.

Four years later, Adolfo invited me to Argentina and returned the favor in a way I never expected.

Adolfo Cambiaso at full gallop.

Argentina, recognized as the world's polo capital, is home to Palermo, often called the Yankee Stadium of polo. Situated in downtown Buenos Aires, this famous venue hosts the legendary Argentine Open, or 'el Abierto,' considered the most prestigious polo tournament in the world.

Adolfo invited my son Chris and me to Buenos Aires to compete in the Masters Cup at Palermo. Only twelve Americans had ever set foot on that sacred ground for a match.

Chris and I were both U.S. Open champions. Yet we felt humbled as we rode onto the lush field that had hosted polo's greatest names: Juan Carlos and Alfredo Harriott, Alfonso and Gonzalo Pieres, and the legendary Heguys. To this day, Chris says that when a mallet strikes a polo ball at Palermo, it produces a unique sound, unlike any echo from other fields. Unforgettable.

Chris still talks about it today: "The green grass inside that concrete jungle of downtown Buenos Aires is like going to Augusta and walking the Masters. It's just beautiful, as perfect a polo venue as has ever been created."

The final pitted our team — Adolfo, Lolo, Chris, and me — against polo royalty: Facundo Pieres, Gonzalito Pieres, Pablo McDonough, and their sponsor, Carlos Reyes Terrabusi.

Tommy Lee Jones, Lolo Castagnola, Adolfo Cambiaso, and Tim Gannon in Outback jerseys.

As excited as I was to play in the Masters Cup with my son, I knew that having both of us on the same team was a significant disadvantage. Our opponents had three professionals; we had only two. The odds were stacked against us, which is precisely when Adolfo plays his best. And that day, so did I.

Not only did we win the Masters Cup, but I was named goleador, the highest-scoring player on the field.

In polo, the patron funds the team. The patron pays the professionals, buys the horses, and earns a spot in the lineup. The patron does not outscore the professionals. That is not how the game works. The goleador is always a pro.

But not on this day!

That was my last match. I left the sport at its peak, standing victorious in polo's sacred cathedral, with my son by my side and my dear friend, Adolfo Cambiaso. There was no better way to say goodbye.

As I moved away from the field, I realized my journey was not over. Polo had given me friendship, family, and purpose, but life still held unforeseen adventures.

Soon, I would find myself immersed in a world of royalty and unexpected friendships.

Nineteen

Royal Treatment

Adventure. No word in English captures it better. I have spent my whole life pursuing it: seeking something new, daring, so far off the beaten path that no one expects it. That craving has never left me.

But I never anticipated this specific adventure: I became good friends with Prince Charles, the future King of England. Have I mentioned how lucky I am?

The journey began in 1998. After a successful high-goal season in South Florida, a friend from England reached out with an intriguing request. "Would you have any interest in playing in a fundraiser at the Royal Military Academy Sandhurst?" The event would benefit the British Forces Foundation, one of the many charities supported by the Prince of Wales.

My response took only a few seconds. Yes, I would love to support the British Forces Foundation. But I had a counteroffer: I would bring Adolfo and Lolo to join me. With two of the world's top polo players on the field, would the Prince of Wales consider playing in the match?

I figured this was a long shot, but I have always loved to swing for the fences. If I strike out, at least I gave it my all.

The answer came: Yes, Prince Charles would love to play.

That single match launched a decade-long tradition. Every summer in England, I played polo with Prince William, Prince Harry, and some of the world's best players. Adolfo was usually on our team. When he could not make it, Memo or Carlos Gracida stepped in. Both were favorites of the Royal family. The legendary Donoso brothers from Chile, Gabriel and Jose, also joined us for many of these matches.

Over the decade, I played in roughly ten matches with the Prince of Wales. Each event supported charities close to his heart: the Riding for the Disabled Association, the Military Benevolent Fund, and the British Forces Foundation, the UK equivalent of the U.S.O.

At Sandhurst, King Charles was at ease. Away from the spotlight and surrounded by loved ones, he was personal and genuine. Our conversations gave me a side of him that few see.

The Prince of Wales was always kind to my children and siblings, treating them with warmth. Each visit to England felt dreamlike, and the memories stayed with us long after we returned home.

But what touched me most came weeks later, after our first match: a handwritten note from King Charles, thanking me for my support. I was stunned. In a world of assistants and secretaries, he had taken the time to write it himself. That first note was just the beginning. Without fail, one arrived after every match. His gratitude was always sincere, his words personal. Those notes meant more than he probably knew.

One year, I gifted him a pair of classic English cavalry spurs crafted from solid silver. From that day forward, he wore them every time we played at Sandhurst.

Polo was only part of it. On one visit, my family received a private tour of the Houses of Parliament from the Speaker of the House of Commons himself.

"Gannon, party of eight from the Colonies," announced the speaker's assistant as we entered his chambers.

Our host, Lord Bernard Weatherill, was British charm personified. He came from a long line of Savile Row tailors, and that refinement showed in everything he did. His dry wit kept us laughing. His journey from tailor to Speaker of the House reflected his integrity and wisdom.

He also shared two stories with us.

Initially, in the House of Parliament, a white line marks the carpet. He explained that the phrase "to toe the line" originates from the line that British parliamentarians were forbidden to cross. It was as if they carried a sword, permitted in the parliament at that time, and could not reach their opponent without crossing that white line.

Lord Wetherall also shared another expression from the House of Parliament: "It's in the bag." Behind the Speaker, there's actually a linen bag where, after a law is voted on or legislation becomes law, it is inscribed on parchment and then placed in it. The phrase "it's

The King and I.

in the bag" originates from the practice of placing the inscribed law in the bag behind the Speaker.

It is very interesting that our expressions today come from the House of Parliament.

Lord Weatherill's ability to blend personal heritage with global experience made him a truly memorable host and companion.

Lord Weatherill attended every one of my polo matches in England. His tours of Parliament were unforgettable. He knew every corner of that historic building and every story behind its art, architecture, and statues.

I had visited Hyde Park many times, but I had never entered the Hyde Park Barracks, home to the Household Cavalry and the leg-

With King Charles.

endary Cavalry Blacks, the Queen's majestic horses. They serve as the Sovereign's Escort during Trooping the Colour, the grand annual celebration of the monarch's official birthday.

Watching the Cavalry Blacks during Trooping is impressive. But I did not just watch. I rode one.

What an unforgettable experience. When Chris and I arrived at Hyde Park Barracks that afternoon, we were first given a riding test to prove we could handle the horses. As U.S. Open champions, we passed with ease.

After demonstrating our skills, we were each assigned a mount. These horses were so large that it felt like climbing onto an elephant. We rode in formation behind the cavalrymen into Hyde Park, the ground shaking with each thunderous hoofbeat.

I quickly realized that the massive horse beneath me had no mouth, as horsemen say, meaning no way to communicate which way to go. None of my attempts to turn or slow down worked. Suddenly, we were galloping at full speed.

I can only imagine how challenging it must be to join a parade, helmets on, shields and swords in hand, while trying to control such powerful, headstrong animals. As a polo player and horseman, I gained immense respect for everyone in the regiment.

For the record, Chris and I both stayed on our galloping giants.

After we had survived the ride, we met for dinner in the Officers' Mess, the regiment's private dining hall.

The Household Cavalry maintains a proud tradition: upon retirement, each officer donates a piece of silver to the Officers' Mess. This custom has endured for centuries. The collection now includes sterling keepsakes, war spoils taken from enemies, donated paintings, and sporting trophies.

Chris and I were dining with silverware that is centuries old, some of it gifted by Admiral Nelson himself. For those who are unaware, Nelson was the famous British naval officer who won victories during the French Revolutionary and Napoleonic Wars.

Of all my trips to England, one highlight stands out: meeting my driver, Mel Windsor. From my first ride in his Jaguar, I felt like royalty. In conversation, Mel mentioned that he and his wife often visited America, so I asked about his favorite restaurant.

"The Outback Steakhouse. Ever heard of it?" he replied.

His answer thrilled me. But had he researched me? So I decided to test him.

What's your favorite appetizer?" I asked.

"My wife and I love to share the Gold Coast Prawns," he said.

As our conversation continued, it became clear that Mel knew the menu by heart. Eventually, I pulled back my vest to reveal the Outback Polo jersey and told him who I was.

Without hesitation, he picked up his phone to call his wife, excitedly telling her he was giving a ride to the creator of the Bloomin' Onion.

From then on, Mel became a close friend and an essential part of my visits to London.

The silver cavalry spurs gifted to King Charles. He wore them at every match after.

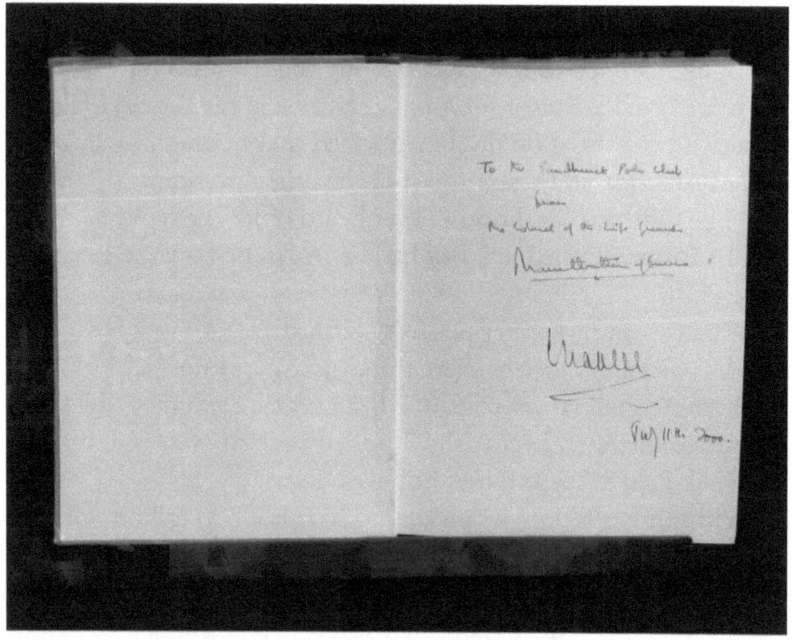

A book inscribed to the Sandhurst Polo Club, signed by King Charles.

HIGHGROVE HOUSE

31st July 2002

Dear Tim,

I could not be more grateful to you for once again coming all the way over from America to support the polo day at Sandhurst. I was absolutely delighted that the total benefit to the charities exceeded £60,000, which will make an enormous difference to their fundraising efforts. It was also a huge pleasure to play with <u>both</u> Memo and Carlos Gracida, whom I have known for so many years, <u>despite</u> William and Harry's apparent best efforts to kill me on the polo field! I do hope that you, too, enjoyed the day and found it all worthwhile.

This comes with my warmest good wishes and heartfelt thanks for your continuing generosity and kindness.

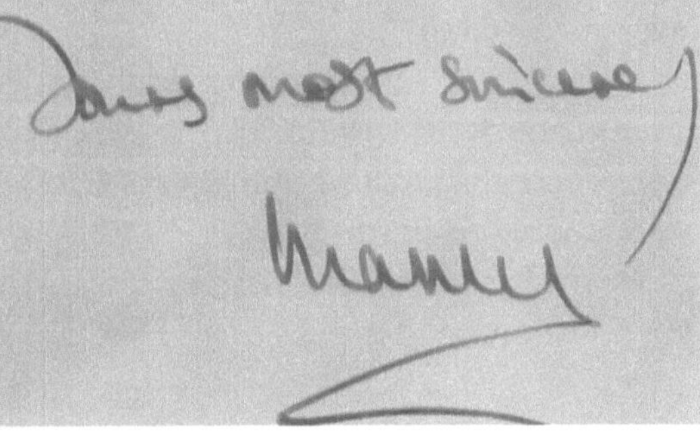

A letter from King Charles on Highgrove House letterhead.

A letter from Buckingham Palace. No stamp required.

One year, my schedule became so packed that making it to the polo match at Sandhurst seemed almost impossible. The day before, I had to attend an Outback Steakhouse board meeting in Pebble Beach, California.

To arrive on time for the throw-in, every connection and transfer had to go smoothly, executed with military precision.

With my assistant Sheryl Fisher's precise itinerary in hand, I sprang into action as soon as the board meeting ended. Outside, my car was waiting. I jumped in, and we zoomed to Monterey Regional Airport.

With no time to spare, I hustled to my gate, caught the flight to San Francisco, then sprinted through the terminal to catch my redeye to London.

At Heathrow, I quickly cleared customs. Mel was already waiting at the curb with the engine running. I threw my bags in the trunk, jumped into the backseat, and just as I closed the car door and clicked my seatbelt, Mel hit the gas.

We sped down the M3, heading toward the Royal Military Academy Sandhurst faster than ever. That day, speed limits were mere suggestions.

As we left the chaos of London behind, the scenery quickly shifted from city to countryside, and I found myself thinking about the journey that brought me here.

It felt like another lifetime since my college days, when I first arrived in London by train from Italy. Back then, I stayed in the East

End at Mrs. Pister's for a dollar a night, sharing a room with several friends. A world away from the car rushing toward Sandhurst now.

Now, flying first-class into Heathrow with a chauffeur taking me to Sandhurst for a polo match with the King Charles, I was living a life I could hardly have imagined years earlier.

Despite the stark differences between these experiences, one humble and the other luxurious, I realized I enjoyed them equally.

Every journey follows its own path, from the thrill of rebuilding my '57 Chevy convertible's engine in Vero Beach with Phil and Johnny to the cherished memory of sharing lunch with Luciano Pavarotti in Italy. Although the two experiences could not be directly compared, they shared a core truth: both were priceless.

Success has a way of opening doors you never expected. Some of those doors led to polo fields in England and Argentina. Others led me to a place I never anticipated: a tiny Caribbean island owned by one of the world's most remarkable entrepreneurs.

For ten consecutive years, I competed in the Necker Cup, Sir Richard Branson's annual pro-am tennis charity tournament on his private island. The guest list read like a who's who of the tennis world: Bjorn Borg, Rafa Nadal, Martina Navratilova, and Stefan Edberg. Richard himself played for two to three hours a day and made sure every guest felt welcome.

In one of those years, American professional Vince Spadea and I competed against Rafa Nadal and his amateur partner, Bill Powers. In my ninth year, British professional Harriet Dart and I won the Necker Cup.

What struck me most was watching Rafa on the practice court. I had seen that same obsession before in Adolfo on a polo field. The sport was different, but the drive was identical. Greatness, I realized, is not tied to any one arena. It lives in a certain kind of person. You recognize it the moment you are in the same room with it.

Yet every one of those journeys had a destination in mind.

Polo had opened doors I never imagined: England with King Charles, Spain for the Gold Cup, and Argentina for the greatest tournament on earth. But those trips always had a purpose, a match to win, a trophy to chase, and a schedule to follow. I wanted to know what would happen if I simply went, with no plan at all.

Martín Valent was one of my earliest grooms, arriving from Ar-

With Rafa Nadal at the Necker Cup on Richard Branson's island.

gentina around the year 2000 with barely a word of English. We taught him the language and helped him learn to manage his finances and taxes. Over time, he became one of my most loyal friends.

One day, I asked him a simple question. "Martín, what are you doing for the next month?"

"Nothing," he said. "I am between jobs."

"Would you like to go around the world?"

He said he would love to.

That was all the planning we needed. No itinerary. No reservations. No agenda. We flipped a coin at every crossroads. Heads, we went east. Tails, we went west. The only rule we made was one we agreed to on the first day: no alcohol for thirty days. This would be a journey of pure adventure, not a vacation. We would treat it like a spa expedition, waking up early, working out, scuba diving, swimming, surfing, and playing polo wherever we could find a field and a horse.

Our first stop was Australia. A helicopter from Kerry Packer's operation took us into the mountains of New South Wales, where the landscape opened onto a polo farm called Ellerston. The property sat high in the ranges, green and remote, a world away from Florida's coastal flatlands. We played polo there, surrounded by nothing but mountains and sky.

That is where I fell in love with three horses. They were sisters, all three of them, and I knew the moment I rode them that I had to have them. I bought all three on the spot and called Phil.

"Phil, I just bought three horses in Australia," I said. "I leave it to you to get them back."

Phil never asked a single question. He simply figured it out and delivered all three horses from the other side of the world to our barn in Florida. That is Phil Heatley.

From Australia, we flew to Thailand. We spent our days scuba diving off Phuket's reefs, exploring the coastline, and pushing ourselves physically in every way we could. At night, we treated ourselves to three-hour Thai massages, unwinding from the day's adventures before falling asleep and doing it all again the next day.

After Thailand, we landed in Dubai, where the polo world has deep roots and deep pockets. We met polo people, played matches, and experienced a city that seemed to have been built overnight from nothing but sand and ambition.

From Dubai, we traveled to India, a country that holds a special place in polo's history. Maharajas played the sport for centuries before it reached England. Walking those grounds and meeting the people who carry that tradition felt like touching the origins of everything I love about the game.

Our final stop was London, which I have always considered the most civilized city in the world. We visited polo friends, went to the theater, and spent our last days abroad savoring the pleasures of a city I had come to know well through my years playing at Sandhurst.

Then we flew home.

It was a freelance adventure with a very good friend. Just the two of us, with nothing specific in mind but to have fun and explore the world. No trophies. No board meetings. No itinerary. Just two men, a coin, and whatever lay around the next corner.

Martín went on to become a five-goal professional polo player, representing Argentina in the 2009 Coronation Cup at Guards Polo Club in England alongside Adolfo Cambiaso and Facundo Pieres. Today, he oversees one of Dubai's premier polo operations. The young man who arrived at my barn, barely able to speak English, became a figure in the international polo world. I like to think our journey together played a small part in that.

When I think about that trip, I realize I captured something essential about how I have always lived. Ever since I was three years old and climbed out the back window of my mother's station wagon, I have had a thrill for adventure, a thrill for exploration, and a thrill at seeing what is out there waiting to be discovered.

Adventure was the constant, the driving force behind my dreams and the reason I said yes to the unknown. Before long, it would lead me to one of the most unlikely friendships I would ever experience.

Charity match at the Royal Military Academy Sandhurst.

Before a match in England.

With Prince William, Jose Donoso, and Chris before a match at Sandhurst.

Prince William, Chris, and Jose Donoso.

A bump with Prince Harry during a match as he sneaks into a mid-goal swing.

With King Charles and Carlos Gracida at Sandhurst.

Twenty

The Power of Giving

I first saw the power of giving through my grandfather, Howard Brundage. It was not just his generosity that shaped me; it included the house, the cars, and my sisters' college tuition. It was the joy it brought him. He taught me that giving itself is a gift.

After Outback went public and my bank account grew, I followed my grandfather's example. I built my mom a house on Longboat Key in Florida. The highlight was the one thing she wanted most: a white couch. White couches and six kids do not mix, but this house was hers and hers alone. She loved it.

Toward the end of her life, she suffered a series of debilitating strokes. My sister Kathy and her husband Jim kindly took her in, and I arranged for her to receive 24-hour care. Knowing that her final days were made comfortable by the success I had worked so hard for still fills me with pride.

As my family expanded and achieved new milestones, I took great joy in supporting their dreams, mirroring my grandfather's example. Motivated by his contributions to my sisters' college education, I was proud to assist my niece, Jennifer Briggs, during her undergraduate studies at Boston College. Seeing her excel as a lawyer has been truly fulfilling.

I also wanted to create unforgettable experiences for my loved ones. I took my brothers and sisters to England, where I introduced them to King Charles, toured the Tower of London, and stayed at The Ritz. Knowing how much my sister Beth adores Barack Obama, I sent her and a friend to his inauguration in Washington, D.C., a memory she still treasures.

I once invited my entire family, including my brothers and sisters and their children, to go skiing in Aspen. Each family member found an Outback Steakhouse ski jacket embroidered with their name in

Surprising Mom with a new car.

their hotel room. Many people, on or off the slopes, mistook us for a ski team, and in many ways, we really were. We have been a team since childhood, united by laughter and shared memories in that old family home.

Giving back to family was personal. But the culture of giving that Chris, Bob, Trudy, and I built into Outback ran far deeper than any of us had imagined. We saw it most clearly when catastrophe struck.

On September 11, 2001, the Twin Towers collapsed, and everything around Ground Zero went dark. Restaurants closed. Supply lines shut down. The city was in shock. Within three days, without a single directive from the corporate office, Outback employees and managing partners in the New York region assembled on their own. They organized like a well-oiled machine, as if they had been doing this for decades. Overnight, they built a kitchen from scratch.

They brought in gas grills. Our suppliers donated the food. Our employees and partners volunteered their time. The New York Fire Department, which knew our company well, escorted propane tanks into the restricted zone, a privilege granted to almost no one else. Outback was one of the few organizations authorized by the NYPD, the fire department, and the mayor to cook at Ground Zero.

Every day, they fed tens of thousands of rescue workers and volunteers. They packed sandwiches into the same buckets used to carry debris down from the pile, so volunteers in line could eat without losing their place. The demand to help was so overwhelming that if a volunteer stepped out of line, someone else would immediately take the spot. A hot meal meant a volunteer could stay in place and keep working.

Over three weeks, Outback served hundreds of thousands of meals at Ground Zero. Not a dollar was charged, and none was asked for. The food and labor were donated, and the spirit behind it was something no one had to teach. It was already part of the culture.

I am proud that Outback was there, and I am proud that the people who made it happen did so because they wanted to, not because anyone told them to.

What happened at Ground Zero was not a one-time event. It was the beginning.

General Tommy Franks, who served on the Outback board of directors, stood up during a board meeting and challenged us to deliver great meals to American soldiers serving in Afghanistan. If we were willing, he said, he could make it happen: military transport, safe delivery of the food, and guaranteed safety for every volunteer.

We were willing.

Outback flew into Afghanistan and fed 50,000 soldiers. Not field rations. Not cafeteria food. Twelve-ounce steaks, grilled lobster, and the Bloomin' Onion. Everything they loved about Outback back home, delivered to Afghanistan. The look on a soldier's face when that plate was set in front of him was something no one who witnessed it ever forgot.

Everyone who made the trip was a volunteer, and the waiting list grew longer each year. There was simply no room. So they waited for the following year, and the year after that. The experience was that meaningful, not just for the soldiers but also for the volunteers who served them.

We did this for nearly ten years.

One of those volunteers was my brother, Pete. Pete is a United States Marine who served in Vietnam, and his esprit de corps has never faded. He brought an American flag to Afghanistan and had it raised there. For Pete, this was not just an Outback trip. It was personal. He stood with his fellow servicemen and women, doing what Marines do: showing up when it matters.

Watching my brother take part in that mission reminded me of why we built Outback the way we did. The principles we lived by were not just words on a wall. They showed up at Ground Zero. They showed up in Afghanistan. They showed up because the people of Outback believed in them.

That spirit of giving did not come from nowhere. It was built into Outback from the beginning, and the man who inspired much of it was Norman Brinker, who had influenced my career more than anyone else.

When Norman passed away, I knew I had one more gift to give to this great man.

As I drove through downtown Dallas, I quietly rehearsed the words I would soon deliver. It was June 16, 2009, and in just a few hours, I would speak at Norman Brinker's funeral before 5,000 of his colleagues, friends, and family. My mind kept returning to the legacy of this legendary restaurateur.

Norman had built an empire, including Steak and Ale, Bennigan's, and more than 1,500 Chili's restaurants. However, as I headed to the Myerson Symphony Center for his Celebration of Life, my thoughts were not on his professional accomplishments. Instead, I reflected on what he meant to me. Norman was not just a mentor; he also motivated me to co-found Outback Steakhouse, create the Bloomin' Onion, and pursue a polo career.

I would speak immediately after Ross Perot, the former presidential candidate and Texas businessman.

Norman pioneered modern casual dining, from the salad bar to how servers introduce themselves. He believed these innovations would foster a warmer, more relaxed atmosphere, and they did. But his most meaningful influence on me was personal.

Years earlier, while in Florence, Phil had described Norman with admiration that bordered on awe. "This man is extraordinary," he said. "He plays polo and owns hundreds of restaurants. His career has given him the freedom to pursue his passions fully." Those words planted a seed that grew into my life's ambition.

Norman was extremely risk-averse in business, but on the polo field, he became the boldest risk-taker I have ever known. Our shared passion for polo strengthened our friendship over the years and forged a lasting bond. When Norman passed away, that bond led me to be there for him one last time, serving as one of the six pallbearers at his funeral.

Polo pulses with adrenaline, with riders perched more than six feet above the turf, racing across the field on horses weighing over a thousand pounds and capable of reaching over 35 miles per hour. The thunder of pounding hooves, the swing of mallets, and the constant tension of sharp turns and dramatic collisions fill the air. This mix of danger and skill draws many to polo's allure.

General George Patton, himself a talented polo player, once said, "The element of personal risk is not a drawback but a decided advantage." In polo, the fearless find the greatest reward.

Severe accidents in polo often occur when two half-ton horses collide at full speed. When a horse falls sideways, the rider can become trapped in the saddle, allowing the animal to land on top of him, resulting in injuries such as broken bones, crushed pelvises, and head trauma. Every polo player acknowledges this risk whenever they mount up.

On January 21, 1993, Norman played for his Chili's team in the Challenge Cup at Florida's Palm Beach Polo and Country Club. In a late-game play against Cadillac, he and an opponent galloped at about 25 mph. As Norman leaned right to strike the ball, he pulled back his mallet, just as the other rider's horse collided with him from the side. Norman never saw it coming.

Norman and his horse toppled sideways, drawing a gasp from the crowd. Norman hit the ground, the right side of his head striking the grass and rendering him unconscious. Seconds later, the rival rider and horse fell on top of him. The other horse struggled to rise but collapsed again on Norman, breaking multiple ribs.

Suddenly, the match ground to a halt as players, officials, friends, and staff rushed to Norman's aid. His wife, Nancy, initially frozen in shock, ran to him. "My God! He's not breathing!" she cried. A medic administered oxygen, and Norman began breathing again. Just four minutes after his collapse, he was being transported, still unconscious, to Wellington Regional Hospital.

Norman sank into a deep coma. A few hours later, Ross Perot, a close friend of Norman, called Nancy. "How is he, Nancy?" Perot asked.

"Oh, Ross," she said. "I am looking at him right now through the window. He has not moved at all since we got here a few hours ago. They have all these tubes hooked up to him. It just doesn't look very good."

Perot tried to calm her. "Don't worry about a thing. I'll take care of it."

Perot promptly contacted Dr. Phil Williams, one of Dallas's top neurosurgeons, and asked him to care for Norman. He informed Williams that his private jet was ready and waiting. Within an hour, the doctor was airborne, bound for Florida to see Norman.

Although Norman received the best available care, the initial prognosis was grim: Nancy was told, "He may have only four to six days to live."

Norman was a true fighter. Despite suffering 32 broken bones, a three-week coma, and temporary paralysis, he survived. Astonishingly, he was back at work after only four months, walking with a walker. My mentor was incredibly resilient and tough.

In 2004, I organized a celebration for Norman called "A Night in Napa with Norm." Forty of his closest friends and business associates gathered at my Napa Valley home for an elegant sit-down dinner. I flew in chefs from New Orleans to prepare the meal.

At a sixty-foot suede-covered table, we enjoyed a rich buttermilk bisque, followed by a grilled romaine salad with lobster, artichokes, and shiitake mushrooms. The highlight was the main course, presented by Chef George Rhode IV himself.

Chef George recounted: "I marinated double-boned half racks of lamb for two hours before grilling them myself. It was hectic: the fire was hot, I moved between the grill and the elevated shelf, and did a lot of praying. But every rack turned out perfect. It was a miracle."

The evening was unforgettable, featuring exceptional food and atmosphere. During dinner, we rotated seats, allowing each guest dedicated one-on-one time with Norman, who appeared genuinely delighted.

Michael Mondavi, co-founder of the Robert Mondavi Winery, politely declined a seat at the table, opting to serve wine and listen to our stories. His presence as our personal sommelier for three hours added a sense of warmth and friendship to the event.

As the evening drew to a close, Norman pulled me aside. His

voice thick with emotion, he said, "I'm not quite sure why you'd do all this for me, but I really appreciate it. I'll never be able to thank you enough."

With Norman Brinker.

"You have been my inspiration for many years," I responded. "You are the reason I entered the restaurant business and the reason I play polo. You have shaped my life in ways you do not even know."

After we hugged, I felt compelled to give him another gift to express my genuine gratitude for everything he had done for me.

Smiling, I said, "I would love to take you to Italy. I want to show you the school I attended and tell you how I first heard your name from my best friend, Phil Heatley. I want to guide you and Nancy around Florence, show you Michelangelo's David, and share the places that shaped my life."

Years later, I kept that promise. Norman and Nancy joined me on a trip to Italy. Even though he was in a wheelchair and could walk only short distances with a walker, we explored without hesitation. We wandered the historic streets together, sharing stories from my youth and discussing how Norman had shaped my path. This experience was beyond words for me.

Norman passed away in 2009 at the age of 78 due to pneumonia. When asked by a family member to speak at his funeral, I immediately agreed. On a humid June afternoon, I drove through Dallas to attend his Celebration of Life, rehearsing my speech.

As I approached the Myerson Symphony Center, I composed myself. I was one of the few who shared Norman's two main passions: restaurants and polo. That is why the family invited me to speak.

The family asked me to focus on Norman's polo history. I knew this would be difficult. Many in the audience believed the sport had taken a heavy toll on him and that the accident had stolen the vitality that once defined him.

For years, Norman's business partners, friends, and family urged him to stop playing polo. He often showed up at meetings covered in bandages, prompting company leaders to ask, "Why do you keep doing this? All you get is hurt."

What they did not realize was that polo was more than just a hobby for Norman; it was his way of life.

Even after his accident, getting to his seat at a polo tournament was a significant challenge. Every slow, cautious step forced him to lean heavily on his ski poles for support. Still, nothing could keep him from watching.

At an event, I sat beside him and asked, "Norman, if you had the chance to go back, would you still choose to play polo?" He responded without hesitation, "If I could, I would be out there right now. If my body let me, I would play polo until the day I die. I would never stop."

My goal was straightforward: to help Norman's closest friends grasp the passion that polo ignited in both of us. I would continue to do what I have always done:

Speak from the heart.

After Ross Perot's speech, I approached the dais and surveyed the 5,000 prominent leaders from the restaurant and business sectors, as well as his family and friends. While I had addressed large audiences before, this moment felt different. This was Norman.

I glanced at my handwritten notes before setting them aside. Facing the audience, I spoke sincerely from the heart. Emotions overwhelmed me with every word, causing tears to well in my eyes. I took several pauses to compose myself, and this is what I remember saying:

Polo captivates you completely. Norman felt that way about the sport, and so did I.

Through injuries, accidents, and even teeth being knocked out, the devoted polo player will always get back on the horse and charge across the field. I have never found any activity more compelling than polo. Not helicopter skiing, not racing cars, not scuba diving with sharks. Nothing compares.

Why is that?

Because it gets to the heart of a powerful idea: the collective effort and the exhilaration of winning as a team. While individual sports like golf and tennis are enjoyable, they lack the shared thrill of a successful team shot. In golf, you might high-five your caddy, but it is still not a team sport.

The concept of team touches the very essence of life. Why are we here?

To support and uplift one another, be of service, and work as a team to navigate life's highs and lows. You join a team to become something greater than you could alone. When you are ill, who do you depend on? Your family and friends. Without your personal team, life becomes much harder. You especially need a team at the end of life, when you prefer not to face your final days alone, in despair, or without support.

Team, team, team. That is what made polo so alluring to Norman.

Yes, he enjoyed the thrill of the game, its intensity, and the courage it demanded to succeed. But what he cherished most was the camaraderie and fellowship of the team.

Norman always believed that success depends on having a great team. It was the core principle of his business career. By working with others, he created opportunities for people around the world and touched more lives than anyone I have ever met.

He was a man of integrity. He never engaged in shady dealings. He believed in the power and magic of teamwork. That is why he succeeded in business and in polo.

The footprints he leaves behind will never erode. They are the footprints of a giant.

After my speech, I returned to my seat.

As Norman's Celebration of Life drew to a close, six pallbearers, including me, carried his casket from the Myerson Symphony Center. Outside, a hearse waited, its engine running. Together, we carefully slid the casket into the hearse. Norman was on his way to his final resting place.

Driving home from the burial that evening, I fell into the familiar introspection that funerals often bring.

In the soft glow of the Texas evening, my mind drifted to my own journey. In many ways, it mirrored Norman's, proof that I had achieved the American Dream. Though I grew up with humble means and little connection to my dad, I reached my goals for two main reasons:

I seized every opportunity that came my way. And, most importantly, I worked my ass off.

Twenty-One

My Family

My children are the greatest joy of my life. All my accomplishments, including every trophy and every risk I took, pale in comparison to watching them grow into the individuals they are today.

Since becoming a father, my life has found its true purpose. I would protect, support, and be actively present in every stage of my children's lives.

The biggest challenge for anyone pursuing success in business or sports is preventing family from fading amid ambition. The pressure, chaos, and relentless demands can make years disappear in a flash, leaving loved ones behind. I chose not to let my ambition come at the expense of my family.

I was not always the father I aspired to be. There were moments I wished I had been more involved. But I never stopped trying to be better.

Paul Newman inspired me in this regard. I never knew him personally, only admiring him from afar. But three things about him stood out to me.

First, he was an incredibly dedicated family man. No matter how famous he became, his family remained his top priority.

Second, he had a successful career. He was focused, worked hard, and achieved great success in film.

Third, he learned how to give back. Newman's Own began with salad dressings and iced tea, flavors he loved, and he turned it into an industry that keeps giving to this day.

A great family. Career success. Learning to give back. Those three elements were important to me. I wanted all three in my life.

I aimed to be the father I never had, the one I wished for as a boy. More than just providing financial support, I wanted to be a source of love, care, and guidance. Over the years, I grew alongside

With Mom at a polo match in Wellington.

my children, learning patience, presence, and love. Fatherhood is an ongoing journey, and I continually strive to improve.

My oldest, Chris, shares my passion for the restaurant business and polo. We all loved horses when he was growing up, and those early years shaped who he would become. Eventually, he and I became business partners, strengthening our relationship beyond father and son. Watching him build Bolay from the ground up has been one of the great privileges of my life.

My daughter Kathleen excelled as an equestrian. Her fierce independence and love of the equestrian world know no bounds. She is an accomplished jumper rider who shares the same drive and the same refusal to quit that have defined our family. She works hard, runs her own barn, rents out stalls, and generates her own income. She does it all on her own, with no support. What makes me most proud is

A young Chris Gannon.

Kathleen and Chris at Palm Beach Polo after a championship.

her resilience, tenacity, and hard work ethic. That independence is something I admire deeply.

Blake, my middle daughter, was always kind and sweet. She does not want to be rich or famous. She just wants to be a good mother and a good wife. Today, she is a devoted mother to two children, raising them with the same gentle spirit she has always carried. It is in that simplicity that her beauty lies.

JT, still finding his way, is becoming a young man of integrity and potential. He loves tennis and made the varsity team at a young age. He is a straight-A student, bright as can be, and one of the sweetest boys I know. He always wants to do the right thing, and that is his greatest strength. He is still discovering where to focus his many strengths, and when he does, he will accomplish great things. I am very proud of him and excited to see the man he will become.

Shannon, the love of my life, caught my attention the moment I saw her. I knew she was special. I often invented reasons to visit, claiming I had urgent matters to discuss with her boss, just to get a chance to say hello. Unbeknownst to me, she was well aware of my intentions.

Shannon is real and down-to-earth, a caring person who everyone loves and wants as their best friend.

With Blake.

For more than thirty-five years, Shannon has stood by my side as my partner, confidant, and greatest friend. We have shared decades of adventures, from scuba diving in the Bahamas to celebrating birthdays around the world. She was with me when I played polo in Palermo, Argentina, and in England, where I played with King

JT Gannon

Charles and met Prince Harry.

She has become not just the love of my life, but a great mother to my youngest child, JT, fulfilling that role with warmth and love. My children hold her dear, just as I do. Her love and loyalty are the bedrock of our family. She is, and always will be, the love of my life.

When I look at my loved ones, I know why I worked so hard. Everything I built was for their benefit.

As a boy, I was lost, with no father, no direction, and no clear idea of my future. I struggled in school and took on various jobs, delivering newspapers, parking cars, digging pools, and tying rebar, often feeling physically and emotionally exhausted before most kids even learn to drive. I never wanted my children to experience such uncertainty or hardship. I aimed to give them the freedom to choose their own paths. Though money cannot buy happiness, it can open doors to opportunity.

When I look back on my life, the restaurants and trophies fade. What remains are my children. Each of them has shaped me, challenged me, and given me a purpose I could never have found in

With Shannon on the Ponte Vecchio, Florence.

business or sport alone. They have become remarkable individuals, each in their own way. I see pieces of myself in some of them and qualities I admire, but I could never claim them in others. Nothing I have built means more to me than who they have become.

Among my children, Chris is the one whose path most closely mirrors my own. We share a love for the restaurant business and a passion for polo. What began as a father-son relationship has evolved into a business partnership, a bond that deserves its own telling.

With Shannon after a full day chasing the sun.

Twenty-Two

My Rising Son

Chris was never invisible the way I was. While I tiptoed through my youth, unnoticed and reserved, my son seemed born to stand in the spotlight. Even as a boy, he commanded attention without demanding it. His confidence, charisma, and drive were unmistakable, and as he grew, those qualities shaped not only his path but also mine.

What began as a father guiding his son became a true partnership. Chris did not just inherit my passion for building restaurants. He took what I taught him and built something entirely his own.

Working alongside Chris, I discovered I was not only teaching him but also learning from him. Together, we built more than a business. We built a bond.

Chris's journey is defined by resilience and ambition.

We share the same roots but chose different paths. I built Outback to pursue polo. Chris built Bolay to nourish others. The values are the same, but the vision is his own.

At seventeen, Chris rode onto the field at the U.S. Open alongside Adolfo Cambiaso. I watched from the stands, hardly believing my son was competing at the sport's highest level, the one I had chased my whole life.

But after high school, Chris struggled to find his way. He tried the restaurant business as a trainee, working eighty hours a week, and he did not survive the hazing like I did. I told him to go back and get his college degree.

His friend Heath talked him into attending junior college in Tallahassee to improve his grades, a story very similar to mine. Chris was not academically inclined. He was living a glamorous life as a U.S. Open champion, traveling the world and playing polo, but he was not financing his lifestyle.

One day, I went to visit him, and we went to a Florida State game

Chris in the Outback number 1 jersey.

together. Chief Osceola charged onto the field on horseback, no saddle, no stirrups, a flaming spear raised high. The crowd roared. Ninety thousand people rose to their feet.

I looked at Chris and said, "That should be your destiny."

He took me seriously.

For two years, Chris trained for fifteen hours a week on horseback. He did not just jump on a horse and ride off. The training required discipline, focus, and a level of commitment he had never shown before.

Chris Gannon is driving toward the ball.

The horse wore no shoes because Indians did not shoe their horses. Chris wore no spurs because Indians did not use them. On a wet field, a horse without shoes can slip, and there is real danger in that. No one has ever fallen off that horse, and Chris was not going to be the first.

He had to maintain a 3.0 GPA, something he had never achieved before. He had to keep his moral code clean while most college juniors were having their wild times. Any rumors of misbehavior would tarnish Chief Osceola's reputation, and Florida State and the Sem-

With Chris at the polo club, a bond that will last a lifetime.

inole Tribe take that seriously.

He also had to keep his identity secret because if someone found out and tried to cause trouble, it would be a disaster. He navigated it all without a blemish.

The horse was kept on a private farm that no one knew about, and sheriffs escorted it to the stadium for every game.

Before each kickoff, Chris rode Renegade onto the field at full gallop, in front of ninety thousand fans and a national television audience of millions. He carried a heavy spear with its tip wrapped in kerosene-soaked cloth, flames leaping into the night air. He rode to midfield, raised the spear high, and drove it into the ground.

That is the declaration of war, the tradition of Osceola. You declare war on the opposing team, and you do it the right way.

Being Chief Osceola is more than being a mascot. You represent the Seminole Tribe and Florida State University. The university honors that relationship by offering free tuition to all Seminole Indians.

FSU serves as an example of what other schools should do with their mascots: treat them with respect.

I was nervous every time I watched him, but Chris never slipped or faltered. He rode out there and declared war, game after game,

Chris Gannon as Chief Osceola, the Florida State Seminoles mascot.

for two years. That discipline changed him, and the narrow track he had to follow shaped him into the man he would become.

After college, Chris went to work at Truluck's in Austin. He started in the kitchen, just as I had decades earlier. He worked his way up to waiting tables and hosting, learning the business from every angle. Stuart Sargent, my old friend and business partner, owned Truluck's and took Chris under his wing.

In 2016, Chris launched Bolay. We had spent months developing the concept together, testing ideas, refining recipes, and pushing each other to get it right. He was searching for his "Velcro" and found it. Chris saw that people wanted to eat healthy without giving up flavor. Nobody was doing it right.

Bolay lets customers build their own bowls from fresh, bold ingredients, creating a different meal every time that is personal to them. That is what keeps them coming back. By 2021, Bolay had grown to twenty-one locations across South Florida.

In 2020, Ernst & Young named Chris the Entrepreneur of the Year in Florida. I thought back to 1994, when Inc. Magazine honored Chris Sullivan, Bob Basham, and me with the same award. Chris was eleven years old then. Now he had earned the recognition on his own.

After the award, Chris told interviewers that I was the best mentor he could have asked for. When I heard those words, I stopped. No trophy, no championship, no business success had ever moved me like that. My son loved and admired me. Nothing else came close.

People sometimes ask what it is like to work alongside my son. The truth is, I learned to watch from a distance.

I have deep expertise in food flavors and strong ideas about what makes a restaurant work. But each person has to learn these things on their own. You cannot teach your son what makes a restaurant tick. You can only shed light on the stories. He has to discover it on his own terms.

Watching Chris discover what he is good at and what he is not good at has been interesting to observe from a distance. I realized early that I could not be there, pointing out his deficiencies. That is not healthy and does not help him on his journey.

You have to make the journey yourself. If your father is always guiding you through every issue, you never take ownership.

Today, Chris takes full ownership of his mistakes and his successes. The mistakes hurt him deeply. They cost him a lot of money when he grew too fast. But the successes taste very sweet to him because they are his, not mine.

When Impact Wealth Magazine asked Chris for advice to entrepreneurs, he did not hesitate:

"The first thing I would tell any entrepreneur is that hard work beats everything. Talent, ideas, and funding mean nothing if you're not willing to outwork everyone else in the room. Show up earlier, stay later, and be the one who keeps pushing when everyone else is ready to quit. That is not just a cliché; it is the reality of building something that lasts. I have witnessed incredibly smart and talented individuals fail simply because they lacked the drive to persevere through tough times. Conversely, I have seen people achieve success purely because they refused to give up."

Reading those words, I realized my son had taken everything I taught him and made it his own.

Watching my son rise has been the privilege of my life. I see my younger self in him, but sharper, more focused, more certain of where he is going. He is not just continuing my journey. He is building something greater.

Some objects carry the weight of a lifetime. One has been with me since I was a teenager, through every triumph and sacrifice, from Twin Farms to Outback to Bolay. It now rests in the open, waiting for the next person who needs to hear its story.

Chris and his first cup win.

Chris helping with riding boots before a match.

On the sidelines with Chris.

With Chris. Both Ernst and Young Entrepreneurs of the Year.

With Chris, founder of Bolay.

Twenty-Three

The Saddle

What became of the special saddle Bud Heatley gave me, which I sold to cover gas for the drive from Houston to Tampa and bet everything on Outback?

I never stopped thinking about it. That saddle was my karma, the driving force behind my success. I had to get it back.

After Outback went public and I finally had the resources to pursue polo, I tracked down Bill Lund. He still owned my saddle.

At the time, Bill owned an air conditioning company in Houston and was an aspiring polo player. When he heard I wanted the saddle back, he offered to return it if I could secure air conditioning contracts with Outback for his company.

I told him that it was impossible. We already had contracts in place, and he was a small regional operation that could not handle the demand.

So I made him another offer. I would buy him the best saddle money could buy, state-of-the-art and brand-new. He tried to negotiate. Finally, I said, "I am coming to get the saddle, and I will give you $1,200, which is four times what I originally paid, but I am coming to get it."

I believed the saddle belonged to me. It was important to me to have it back. He eventually recognized its significance to me and sold it to me for $1,200.

When I finally held it again, everything fell into place. I had the success of Outback. I had the saddle Bud gave me all those years ago, the one he handed me with the words "Put it to good use." It was my karma. With this saddle in my hands again, I felt complete. The journey had come full circle.

Today, it is displayed at Bolay's corporate headquarters, not behind a glass case but out in the open. Chris encourages every Bolay

Damian Mendola - Cofounder of Carrabba's Italian Grill

team member who passes by to reach out and tap it for good luck.

That saddle is more than leather and stitching. It is the price I paid to start over and the risk I took when I had nothing left to lose. Now it belongs to Chris and to everyone at Bolay who needs a reminder that big lives begin with a single, terrifying leap.

Over the years, I learned that the right partners can take any idea further than one person ever could. Johnny Carrabba brought a small Italian restaurant to Outback. We partnered with him, and Carrabba's Italian Grill grew into something neither of us could have built alone. Paul Fleming had a vision for an upscale steakhouse. We believed in him, and Fleming's Prime Steakhouse became a nationwide success. The founders of Bonefish Grill had two or three restaurants in St. Petersburg. They partnered with us, and suddenly, they had 200.

The common thread is not the concept. It is the people. When I look back at times when I was unsuccessful, the problem was almost always the same: I did not have the right partners. And when I look at others who could have been even greater, like Al Copeland or Norman Brinker, brilliant men who never fully embraced sharing equity, I see what they left on the table.

Sharing equity was our secret weapon. It attracted talent. It kept talent. And it pushed that talent to stretch further than they ever imagined.

People often ask me about risk. They see the adventures, the bull, the polo, the motorcycle ride across Africa, and assume I have no fear. That is not true. I feel fear like anyone else. The difference is what I do with it. I sold a saddle that meant everything to me, and I have said yes to things that terrified me.

The goal is to be fearless without being reckless. It is as simple as that.

When I rode a motorcycle from London across Africa, I always wore a helmet. I was a defensive driver and always careful. The motorcycle was the only affordable way to go on that adventure, but I never treated it as an excuse to be careless.

When Chris Sullivan invited me to go helicopter skiing, I said yes. Chris is fearless, too. He loves snow skiing and wanted to share this experience with me. I could ski well enough, but the people who go on these helicopters are a different breed. They are usually National Ski Patrol members who do this kind of thing because it is insane, the views, the rush, all of it.

So I went. I was forty-five years old.

The helicopter drops you on top of a mountain with about ten feet of powder on the surface. Below that, cliffs. You are with eight guys who can ski anywhere and through anything. They put one instructor in front and one in back to help you through.

It was one of the scariest things I have ever done.

About sixty percent was gorgeous, just sailing through ravines with views you cannot imagine. Another ten percent was undoable. You had to take your skis off and walk across streams, rivers, and rocks. And then there was the other twenty percent where I looked down and said, I cannot do this.

The ski patrol guy said, "Well, it is the only way down. There is no other way."

So I did things I thought I could never do. Flipping from one ski, cutting back and forth, all the way down. When I finally made it, it was glorious. But frightening. About twenty percent of that mountain was way beyond my ability. Not for those guys. They handled it easily. But they put up with me.

I was the last guy into the helicopter and the first guy out. That was rough. The helicopter ride to the top took about five minutes, so you got five minutes of rest between runs. Normally, at a ski resort, the lift ride is forty minutes up and forty minutes down. This was five minutes up and one hour down. Intense does not begin to describe it.

I would never do it again. But I am glad I did it.

I am glad I fought a bull. I am glad I rode across Africa. I am glad I played polo against the world's best players.

Life gives you windows of opportunity. You either do something or you do not. At the end of your life, you look back on two lists: the things you did not do that you are glad you skipped, and the things you did that you are glad you tried, even when they were scary. The more of those adventures you take on, the ones where you went ahead and did it anyway and got through them, the richer your life becomes.

But do not be reckless.

In polo, I never put myself in a position to be reckless. I always knew which plays could work and which would not. If I went into a play where I did not belong, bad things would happen. The people who get racked up with broken ribs and shattered bones are the ones who go into plays they have no business attempting.

Fearless, not reckless. That is the line I have walked my entire life.

The lessons I have learned in my life always go back to the low points.

I think of sitting in the dugout during Little League, watching my teammates take the field without me. I wanted so badly to be out there. To play. To compete. To win. To be part of a team.

I learned how to get out of that dugout. I learned how to find the right partners, build the right teams, and chase dreams that once seemed impossible.

But here is what may be more rewarding than the trophies, the cups, and the victories: do not forget to send the elevator back down.

By that, I mean bring along the people who helped you get through life. Lift them up as best you can so they can find the same joy and achievement in their lives as you found in yours.

These days, I make weekly visits to my local Outback. I have gotten to know the staff by name, and sometimes I tell them the story of how it all began.

When I officially retired from Outback and gave up my stock, I received a parting gift: a $100 card redeemable at any Outback Steakhouse worldwide, valid for every visit, for life. That card has become one of my most treasured possessions.

Not long ago, I pulled out of my driveway and headed to the local Outback. A cheerful waitress smiled as she handed me my order. I showed my loyalty card, tipped her well, and eagerly opened my meal.

It was perfect, just as I had imagined it all those years ago. I raised a petal of the Bloomin' Onion to my mouth. Everything I had worked for, right there in a single bite.

With every bite, the memories came back. Bud's ranch. The first time I saw the Onion Mum. When Chris, Bob, and Trudy raised their glasses on opening night. All of it, right there in my hands.

What seemed like a simple dish had been a loyal companion through many stages of my journey. The Bloomin' Onion took me on an incredible adventure, and I am forever grateful for all the good it has brought me.

The saddle at Bolay and the Bloomin' Onion at Outback remind me that life is not just about what we build, but also about what we pass on.

And I am not finished.

Looking back, I realize that what stays with you is not the trophies, the IPOs, or the number of restaurants you open. What you remember are the friendships, especially those forged when you are at your lowest. I remember all the people who came to my rescue when I was down and out. There have been many.

You may not remember everyone you helped along the way, but you will always remember the people who helped you. Those memories are the dearest and sweetest of your entire life.

That is why I wrote this book. I wanted to share these lessons in the best way I knew how: through a story, an adventure you could enjoy and learn from at the same time.

If my journey helps even one person find their why, discover their Velcro, or take a leap toward the life they desire, then it will have been worth every page.

Twenty-Four

Epilogue

At a recent fundraising auction, I offered to cook my signature dish for the highest bidder: the Bloomin' Onion, the appetizer I created decades ago in a Tampa kitchen. Paddles instantly flew up around the room.

Ten strangers pooled their resources. Two thousand dollars each. Twenty thousand dollars for a single appetizer.

I stood there, taking it in. A single dish had just moved ten strangers to give twenty thousand dollars. The Bloomin' Onion had become more than a dish. It had become a reason to gather, give, and connect.

Watching those strangers celebrate together, I thought of my mother. She used to tell me the story of Achilles: how his mother dipped him in the River Styx to make him invincible, but the heel she held remained dry. That one vulnerable spot became his undoing.

My mother believed everyone had an Achilles' heel. She was sure she knew mine: relentless optimism.

"You see the best in everything, even when you should not," she would say, half worried, half amused. To her, my hope was dangerous. It would blind me to reality and lead to my downfall.

Life proved her wrong.

At fifteen, I was tying steel rebar under the Louisiana sun, wondering whether I would ever escape that life. A year later, Bud Heatley handed me a polo saddle and told me to put it to good use. Twenty years later, Chris Sullivan handed me a partnership and told me to do the same.

My optimism never let me down. It drove me forward.

The trait my mother feared would destroy me became the engine of everything I built. It helped me see an opportunity where others saw only risk. When Chris Sullivan wrote me a ten-thousand-dollar check to become his partner, he was betting on that optimism. So was I.

I did not write this book to impress you with trophies or restaurants. I wrote it because I know what it feels like to wonder whether your dreams are foolish. They are not.

There were nights when I wondered if I was fooling myself. Nights when the debt piled up, and the dream felt impossibly distant. But I kept going. That is all any of us can do.

That evening, watching ten strangers celebrate an appetizer I invented in a Tampa kitchen, I understood something. My mother had it backward. Optimism was never my weakness. It was my greatest gift.

If a 15-year-old tying rebar in Louisiana dirt can help build Outback Steakhouse, play polo with a future king, and win his final match at Palermo with his son at his side, then your dream is closer than you think.

Send the elevator back down. That is what Chris Sullivan did for me. That is what Bud Heatley did for me. Now it is my turn.

About the Author

Tim Gannon scoring the winning goal in the Spanish Gold Cup.

Tim Gannon is the co-founder of Outback Steakhouse and the creator of the Bloomin' Onion, the best-selling appetizer in casual dining history, with over $1 billion in sales.

What began as a single restaurant on a side street in Tampa in 1988 has grown into more than 1,000 Outback Steakhouse locations across more than 20 countries. Tim and his partners also helped build Carrabba's Italian Grill, Fleming's Prime Steakhouse and Wine Bar, and Bonefish Grill, all under the Bloomin' Brands umbrella, a company named after Tim's signature creation.

Tim grew up as the son of a single mother raising six children in Fort Lauderdale, Florida. He began delivering newspapers at nine, tying rebar in pool ditches at fifteen, and parking cars at sixteen. He earned a B.A. in Art History from Florida State University, studying abroad in Florence, Italy, where he led tours at the Uffizi Gallery and was awarded the Florentine fleur-de-lis by the Mayor of Florence for his service as an ambassador of American tourism.

At age forty-two, Tim began playing polo. Within a decade, he founded the Outback Polo team, which Rolex named the world's number-one team. He went on to win five U.S. Open Polo Championships, competing alongside legends such as Adolfo Cambiaso and Memo Gracida.

Tim was named Ernst & Young Entrepreneur of the Year alongside his partners, Chris Sullivan and Bob Basham. He lives in Wellington, Florida.

Tim is available for keynote speeches, fireside chats, and motivational speaking engagements. To book Tim, visit OutbackTim.com.

Acknowledgements

Shannon, the love of my life, what can I say? You know all my faults, yet you smile when you see me. I truly love you for that, for everything you have been to my family, and for how you consider them your family. Thank God for how they consider you their mom.

Mom, thank you for bringing me into this world. Thank you for teaching me to earn my money from my brain, not my back. It took a little time to learn that, but I got it. Thank you for everything and for being a special mom to six wonderful children.

Beth, the oldest, you have always been our family's caretaker, the one who ensures everyone is okay. You always check on everyone. Even now, at 84, you think of everyone every day.

Judy, you have always been a great mentor, always there with great advice. Your commitment to health, wellness, and well-being is incomparable. Thank you for being such an inspiration.

Kathy, may you rest in peace. You were my dolly. You were the one who watched out for me and created a great family of four daughters and twelve grandchildren. What a wonderful footprint you have left on this world, and this world will never forget you.

Mo, you have always been there for Pete and me, from the early days of cooking our meals when we were fourteen and making sure we were always fed. You have always been there. You are a true and great family member and a wonderful sister.

Pete, you have been the captain of my yacht. You have been the adventure on the high seas, scuba diving with sharks, and keeping me safe under your watchful eye. You have rescued so many people over your lifetime that I cannot begin to count. Your footprint on this planet is strong and well thought out. Thank you, Pete.

Chris, I have loved watching you grow up. I loved you winning the U.S. Open. I loved you as Chief Osceola. You made me so proud. And I love you now as CEO of Bolay. Keep it going. You have the wind at your back.

Kathleen, you are a hardworking, steadfast equestrian and a giant lover of the sport. It is great to see you enrich the equestrian world as your family has.

Blake, you define sweetness. Sweetness is in your DNA. Congratulations to you and your family, and on who you have become.

JT, you are the man. You are the one pulling the caboose, and you are going to make it all happen and make the Gannon name so proud and well recognized once again. The wonderful lady who adorned my apartment with a Christmas tree and gifts when I could not afford them, you are always a sweet memory of a Christmas made possible by a stranger.

Phil Heatley, what a friend you have been, and what an inspiration, to get me out of those pool ditches and into the bright world of Florida State University, Florence, the slopes in Aspen, and especially the polo fields.

Bud Heatley, you are the spirit of polo. You are the one who brought me into the world of polo. From you, I draw the grandeur of the sport.

Norman Brinker, you are the umbrella of the entire casual dining industry. You have spawned so many leaders in the restaurant business. Above all, you have been a true friend to me, and I cherish our memories and our time together, especially in Italy.

Warren Leruth, you are the master of all chefs. You are the one chosen to represent America, and I will always be indebted to you for the guidance you gave me to get it right.

Al Copeland, you are a master of flavor. I came to understand flavor through your eyes and your hard work. We developed so many great dishes together. You taught me about recruiting great chefs, learning from others, and recipes that get it right.

George Rhode IV, you are the best. You have been with me in the trenches through the dark days and in the bright days. We have always endured our friendship through thick and thin. You are a genius at what you do.

Stuart Sargent, you have always been a loyal friend. Through all the ups and downs in the restaurant industry, you have been there, showing your loyalty and your class. You are in a class all by yourself.

Joe Kadow, what a friend you have been through the good times and the hard times, keeping us all in check, keeping us in bounds when we tried to step out of them, and keeping it fun. Especially fun. Your sense of humor has made us laugh through all the years.

Chris Sullivan, thank you for pulling me out of the dugout and onto the field, and for teaching me how to compete in the wonderful world of the restaurant industry.

Bob Basham, thank you for your graciousness, partnership, loyalty, and great common sense. You have always given me great guidance.

Trudy Cooper, thank you for making us all laugh when it was awkward and for making us all smile when it was awkward, too. Thank you for bringing us such joy, keeping everything light and funny, and making this ride such a great laugh.

Billy Rosenthal, you taught me so much about the meat industry, but more than anything, you taught me what a great partner is. A handshake goes a long way with you, and it remains true today in the way we do business. Thank you, Billy.

Ben Rosenthal, son of Billy, those are tough shoes, but you are filling them with pride and grace. You will take Standard Meat Company to new heights.

Sheryl Fisher, you know all my adventures and have been with me through thick and thin. Your sense of humor has carried me through them all.

Adolfo Cambiaso, you are still number one in the world. I met you when you were approaching number one. I was there when you became number one and have stayed number one. I could not be happier with our partnership and our trust in each other to help each other grow and achieve such success together in the polo world.

Mark Cann, thank you for calling me out of the blue and inviting me to play polo at Sandringham with King Charles. I knew immediately that I would love to do it. Thank you for having the instincts to call me and make it all happen, leading to ten great years of polo and a great friendship with His Majesty and the Princess.

Memo Gracida, you are a total master of the sport of polo. Your discipline, knowledge, and attention to detail far exceed those of any other polo player. Thank you for bringing me to the highest level of the game and for helping me win my first two U.S. Opens.

King Charles, it has been such an honor to play polo with you. Your ability to make one feel special has always been evident. Your charm and hospitality to my family and me over the ten years we played together have been incomparable.

John Ingram, some friendships form before two people ever share a room. Through the polo world and through people we both trust, you became someone I knew I could count on. When this book needed a home, you and the Ingram team made the decision an easy one. That kind of loyalty does not come from a contract. It comes from character. I am proud to call you a friend.

Tommy Lee Jones, from the first day I met you, when you barked at me about getting up from the polo field after you knocked me down, we have had fun, and it has been a great ride through the polo fields of England, Argentina, and the United States, and through the islands, scuba diving in the Exumas. You have been a true friend and one of the most interesting polo players in the world.

Steve Harvey, I love you to death. That is all I can say. You remembered me after our radio show, when I told you, "You are going to make it big one day, Steve. And when you do, you call me." You did. You put me on your national television show and made me a TV star.

Don Yaeger, thank you for bringing this book to life and for inspiring the effort to get it underway.

Deyson Ortiz, thank you for coming in at a time when publication of this book was in serious doubt. You took control and made everything happen smoothly and seamlessly. I am forever in your debt.

Amy Cianci and St. Petersburg Press, thank you for working with me to bring this book to print. I appreciate your attention to detail, your honesty, and your transparency throughout the process.

Leigh Pierce, from the very first call, you treated this project as if it were your own. Your knowledge, your patience, and your genuine care for this book made the most daunting parts of publishing feel manageable. You made a complicated process feel like a conversation between friends. Thank you for believing in this story.

Brent Spears, your eye for design gave this book its face. The cover is simple, elegant, and impossible to look away from. You put the Bloomin' Onion at the center, exactly where it belongs, because without it, many of these adventures would not have been possible. We are grateful for your talent and dedication to getting every detail right.

The Ingram team, the people behind the scenes who turn a manuscript into a book on a shelf and into the hands of readers around the world. Your professionalism, your enthusiasm for this project, and your commitment to getting it right have meant everything.

My readers, I hope this book offers insight into a person who had great dreams and struggled to realize them. It was not an easy journey, but it was one filled with great mentors and support along the way. I look back and thank all those who got me out of the dugout and onto the playing field, where I love to compete like nothing else.

A Note from Tim

Thank you for reading my story. I wrote this book because I believe that where you start does not have to determine where you finish. If anything in these pages inspired you, challenged you, or simply made you smile, I would be grateful if you took a moment to share your thoughts with a short review on Amazon. Your words help other readers discover the book and keep the conversation going.

I am also available for keynote speeches, fireside chats, consulting, and speaking engagements. If you think my story could inspire your team, your organization, or your event, I would love to hear from you at OutbackTim.com.

Scan the QR code below to visit the book page, leave a review, or learn more:

OutbackTim.com/book
Thank you for being part of this adventure.
Tim Gannon

OutbackTim.com/book

"Always believe. Always work.
Always dream."

— Tim Gannon